PLENISH.

PLENISH.

juices to boost, cleanse & heal

Mitchell Beazley

Kara M. L. Rosen

An Hachette UK Company
www.hachette.co.uk

First published in Great Britain in 2015 by Mitchell
Beazley, a division of Octopus Publishing Group Ltd
Carmelite House, 50 Victoria Embankment
London EC4Y 0DZ
www.octopusbooksusa.com

Distributed in the US by Hachette Book Group,
1290 Avenue of the Americas, 4th and 5th Floors,
New York, NY 10020

Distributed in Canada by Canadian Manda Group,
664 Annette St., Toronto, Ontario, Canada M6S 2C8

ISBN 978-1-78472-035-3

Printed and bound in China

10 9 8 7 6 5 4 3 2

The information in this book is intended only as a guide
to following a healthy diet. People with special dietary
requirements of any kind should consult appropriate
medical professionals before changing their diet. Whilst
all reasonable care has been taken during the preparation
of this edition, neither the publisher nor author can
accept any responsibility for any consequences arising
from the use of this information.

This book includes juices and dishes made with nuts and
nut derivatives. It is advisable for customers with known
allergic reactions to nuts and nut derivatives and those
who may be potentially vulnerable to these allergies,
such as pregnant and nursing mothers, invalids, the
elderly, babies, and children, to avoid dishes made with
nuts and nut oils. It is also prudent to check the labels of
ingredients for the possible inclusion of nut derivatives.

PLENISH is a registered trademark of Plenish Cleanse Ltd.

Contents

Introduction

Journey to the Juice   6
Kara's "Cabinet"   10
The Knowledge   14

What's Ailing You?   **26**

Arthritis • Constipation • Excess Weight • Fading Fitness Performance • Fertility and Conception • Gout • High Blood Pressure • High Cholesterol • Insomnia • Liver Fatigue • Low Sex Drive • Stress and Adrenal Fatigue • Struggling Skin Health

For the Love of Juice   **54**

When to Juice and When to Cleanse   56
Choosing a Juicer   56
Tips on Buying Produce   57
Ingredient Superstars   58

Juice Recipes   **60**

Sweet and Easy Greens   62
Hardcore Deep Greens   70
Fruits   78
Roots   94
Nutm*lks   102

Once Upon a Cleanse   **108**

What is a Cleanse?   110
The Cleanse Program   112
The PLENISH Pantry Makeover   114
Start Your Pre-cleanse Program   116
It's Cleanse Day!   118
Post-cleanse   120
Cleanse Symptoms   121

Cleanse meal recipes

Breakfast   122
Lunch   127
Dinner   132

Index   **138**

Acknowledgments   **144**

Journey to the Juice

Kara's Story

High times

The year 2007 was an exciting time in New York City. I was in my late 20s, working on the launch of *Men's Vogue* at Condé Nast. The economy was booming and everyone I knew was spending and living large. I traveled quite often to the West Coast for work with my colleagues, where we stayed at amazing hotels with unlimited mini bars on generous expense accounts that allowed us to eat to our hearts' content at the best restaurants. This excess started to take its toll.

As a single 20-something living in a studio apartment in Manhattan, boundaries blurred and discipline dissolved. I suffered from a recurring case of "strep throat" (a streptococcal infection) that my doctor treated each time with antibiotics. I was grateful that popping a few pills and then dealing with the candida infection that came with them provided the quickest route back to work and my social life. I took my dwindling energy levels to mean that I just needed more coffee and a few extra hours of sleep at the weekend to "catch up." But that wasn't fixing it.

I will ~~survive~~ *thrive*

I now call this the walk of the vertically ill — doing what it takes to *survive*, but not enough to *thrive*. I survived on this roller coaster for nearly two years, consuming antibiotics for a total of twelve months over that period. The thing about antibiotics is that they are fantastic at killing bacteria, but they can't discriminate between the good and the bad. So although the antibiotics were destroying all of the bacteria that were causing my strep, they also killed off all the good bacteria, leaving my gut and immune systems in a severely weakened state.

I suffered with bouts of depression, feeling very low and foggy-headed, which I attributed to going through a quarter-life crisis and the fact that I was single and feeling lonely. I no longer had the energy to run and exercise, which had been a regular part of my life and an effective method of relieving stress. What I failed to consider was that something chemical was actually out of whack in my body. Friends and family suggested that I get off my sofa and "go out more" to overcome my fatigue and low spirits. This inevitably led to more drinking and eating the wrong comfort foods, like white bread and pasta and sugary and fried food. What I thought would be a way to beat feeling depressed only made it worse.

Albert Einstein gave me a kick in the a***!

Feverish, lethargic, and feeling depressed (and chubby!), and with strep beating the antibiotics again, I felt I was at rock bottom. I went back to the doctor one final time. In addition to a prescription for a new, stronger antibiotic and the generous offer to remove my tonsils, I was referred to a psychiatrist. Their solution was an antidepressant to help "lift the cloud."

Sitting on the New York subway en route to collecting my prescription, and feeling like I was turning 70 rather than 30, a poster I had probably seen many times before suddenly caught my attention. It featured Albert Einstein's definition of insanity:

Insanity: doing the same thing over and over again and expecting different results.

I felt like Albert was sitting next to me on the train and giving me a kick in the backside from the year 1909. I knew I needed to do something different with my health.

I wish I could have told my younger self then that 95 percent of the happy hormone serotonin is produced in your gut, so looking after your second brain, as I now call my gut, is the first step to mental well-being.

Send me a healer, or some kale, please

I felt the inner physician in me awaken with a new challenge — what changes did I need to make to my life to break this "insane" illness cycle? I didn't know exactly how to find the answer, but on the advice of enlightened, healthy friends, I went to see a naturopath and a nutritional therapist. What blew me away was that, even before the appointment with the nutritional therapist, I was asked to fill out a questionnaire with heaps of questions, 90 percent of which were related to food and diet, and asked to keep a food diary for 10 days. My (what I thought then were mostly healthy) choices looked something like this:

7.30am breakfast: oatmeal made with water, fruit, and a coffee, or peanut butter on toast

1pm lunch: grilled chicken or turkey sandwich (hold the mayo, I'm calorie conscious!)

3pm snacks: frozen yogurt and fruit and, more often than not, a coffee

8pm dinner: some kind of takeaway meal

"Wait, it's 8pm and I haven't had any fresh veggies?" This missing ingredient would play a big role in unlocking my healthy future.

Happy gut, bye bye rut

After various tests that ruled out any food intolerances, the nutritional therapist felt confident that by making some significant changes to my diet, namely cutting back on processed foods and sugar and adding in a lot more living, raw foods that are naturally low in sugar, I could get my strep and candida under control and help lift my mental cloud. Because of the processed convenience foods I was eating, along with regular coffee and wine consumption, my system was quite acidic. Thanks to the antibiotics, I had hardly any good bacteria left in my system to fight off illness, and my second brain (gut) was not in any shape to make enough serotonin to keep my first brain happy. I was hopeful and inspired that my health was in my control, and the solution was as simple as eating more veg and less processed crap.

CTRL + ALT + DELETE and the clean slate

My first prescription from the nutritional therapist didn't involve pills, nor the removal of a body part from my throat. Instead, I found myself embarking on a five-day juice cleanse, to clear out the toxins in my system while flooding my body with living alkaline nutrients (see pages 17–19). I was, and still am, a total foodie, so the thought of replacing solid foods with liquid was quite intimidating, but like Albert Einstein said to me on the subway, I had to do something different if I wanted a different result. So I started my juice cleanse.

The first day? Surprisingly easy. The second day? I had a headache, felt low on energy, and was unsure how I would last the full five days. But I was on a journey and a little juice wasn't going to scare me. So I persevered, and by the end of the third day I had turned a corner. What inspired me to continue was the mental clarity that very quickly returned. I was able to read a full page again without zoning out, and I slept like a baby. Although I missed chewing food, I wasn't hungry, and with every sip of green juice I could start to feel the benefits of my cells booting out the toxins and lapping up vital nutrients. By the end of day five, I felt like I had taken the reins of my health back, and was also psyched about having a flatter, happier tummy.

PLENISH your body and it will heal itself

Cleanse programs tell you how to detox, but what I wanted to know was: what happens next? How was I to ride this post-cleanse wave and use my renewed energy to make some sustainable, lifelong changes to my health destiny? I was empowered to seek a redesign of the rest of my life through my diet, secure in the knowledge that a cleanse would provide a reboot whenever I felt below par. After a few more sessions with the nutritional therapist, and a course of probiotics to get my gut bacteria, or flora, back in sync, I started to heal what I hadn't known was broken and blazed a new life path for myself free from antibiotics, illness, and depression.

I found that when I was feeling good physically, I radiated positive energy and attracted other positive people to me. Once I had healed myself internally, I was able to open myself up to love and intimacy with someone I connected with. I met my husband (and now baby daddy), who is my rock and allows me to be his, too. The knowledge I gained during my journey to the juice inspired me to make permanent changes to my diet to keep me healthy.

When I arrived in the UK in 2009, I couldn't find the vegetable-based juices I had grown to depend on. So I took the bull by the horns and started PLENISH. Now I am writing this book so that you don't have to reach the lows I did, or count on a chance encounter with Albert Einstein to turn your life around!

Find your inner physician

Most of us think of advances in medicine in terms of high-tech surgery with lasers, or a new drug that a pharmaceutical company has spent millions of dollars and years of research bringing to the market. What is hard to believe until you've experienced it yourself is how the power of the simple choices we make in our everyday lives — such as what we eat, how we deal with stress, how often we exercise, and how much love and intimacy we have in our lives — can affect our overall health. Well, it does. Big time.

By reading this book, you've clearly arrived on the brink of your very own health evolution. These pages offer a safe place for you to experiment with creating your own health destiny. So wake up your inner physician and become your own health detective.

Are you living above or below the line?

In today's busy society, many of us are ignoring our body's cues to what it needs. Rather than slow down when we feel fatigued, we press the ignore and override buttons, leaving us running on fumes fueled by coffee, processed sugar, and short-term fixes that continue to steer us further away from our baseline of health. Think about it and ask yourself: are you doing what it takes to *survive*, but not enough to *thrive*?

Your prevention toolkit

People often ask what the story is behind the name PLENISH. To PLENISH is to keep your body ahead of the curve. Rather than rePLENISH, let's put our prevention hats on and empower ourselves to make the necessary changes to avoid the need for replenishment. By feeding your cells and body with what it needs preventatively — the wonderful phytonutrients, vitamins, minerals, and antioxidant power from the fruit and vegetable kingdom — your body can heal itself and, better yet, help prevent any illness down the line.

What I strive to do in this book is to give you the tools to live at and above the baseline of health. When you feel that life's daily challenges are dragging you below the line and you're merely surviving rather than thriving, you now have a guide to rebooting your system, PLENISHing your cells to get you back to your high-performing self.

You are in the driver's seat, and with your new tools and knowledge, you can break bad eating habits before they break you. Buckle your seatbelt, put the pedal to the metal, and get juicing!

To your health,

Kara xx

9

Kara's "Cabinet"

Ever met a one-man band? Me neither. I am well aware that the amount of nutrition and health information out there is absolutely overwhelming. But with this book, I aim to give your inner health problem solver or inner physician the confidence to find the appropriate path to well-being. Rather than seeking a solution in the form of a pill, here you can look to your diet and use plant-based, living foods to treat the root of your health issues.

That said, no matter how clever your inner physician may be, it's impossible to become an expert on every aspect of health and nutrition, so you need people you can trust and rely on to help you on your personal health journey. My advisors on speed dial are featured here — the guys that make up my little green book of top nutrition and wellness stars.

My Little Green Book of Experts

Expert biog 1:
Romina Pulichino

Romina Pulichino is a registered dietitian with a Masters Degree in Business. After concluding her studies in the USA she took a nutrition residency at Harvard Medical School's Brigham and Women's Hospital in Boston, Massachusetts.

Romi has primarily worked in clinical settings caring for patients from different socio-economical backgrounds with a range of medical and nutritional challenges. Her health philosophy is "You are what you eat and what you think."

Romi was an original member of the PLENISH team, overseeing the range, its nutritional value and composition.

Areas of specialty

- Clinical nutrition
- Cardiovascular health
- Metabolic syndrome
- Gastrointestinal health
- Overweight/obesity
- Mindful eating

Twitter: @rominapulichino

Expert biog 2:
Eve Kalinik

Expert biog 3:
Gabriela Peacock

Having graduated with a nutritional therapy diploma from the College of Naturopathic Medicine in London, Eve wanted to help others discover the benefits of eating well and the way nutrition can assist the body's natural healing ability. "I love food. And that's not just about making tasty enjoyable recipes, but also exploring how eating well can make you feel incredible," she explains.

Eve works on an individually tailored approach to develop lifelong plans for eating well. She is not an advocate of calorie restriction but encourages eating nutritional, beneficial, and therapeutic foods to increase vitality and a general consistent feeling of well-being. Eve understands the difficulties and limitations in changing lifestyles, having previously spent almost 15 years in a high-pressure job, and always considers "real life" when devising recipes and nutritional programs.

Eve is passionate about increasing the role of plant foods in the diet and the hands-on side of nutrition. Alongside her practice she also runs interactive workshops, supper clubs and contributes to various publications on healthy eating topics.

Eve has been working with PLENISH clients since 2013 on a one-to-one basis to help them design their healthier and happier future through nutrition-led healing. She also oversaw the pre- and post-cleanse food recipes (pages 122–137).

Areas of specialty

- Gut health
- Skin health
- Stress management
- Recipe development
- Interactive workshops

Website: www.evekalinik.com

Gabriela Peacock has a BSc Hons degree in Health Science (Nutritional Therapy) from the University of Westminster and a Nutritional Therapy Diploma from the College of Naturopathic Medicine (CNM).

A background in fashion modeling enlightened Gabriela about the importance of a nutritious diet and its impact on maintaining a youthful body image. Gabriela believes that certain nutrients and lifestyle practices can nourish our bodies and our lives and can significantly help to maintain wellness, from a youthful body to clearer skin and improved energy levels. She approaches nutrition from a wholefoods perspective, focusing on delivering dietary and lifestyle advice and debunking popular myths propagated by misinformation in the media.

Through the application of nutritional science, Gabriela looks to identify biochemical imbalances that may hamper the attainment and maintenance of optimal health. Working in private practice, Gabriela gives guidance tailored to complement medical treatment and promote health through the provision of nutrient-rich food choices and appropriate supplement protocols.

Gabriela's approach is patient centered and evidence based: she recognizes that each person is an individual, with unique requirements and differing health goals.

Areas of specialty

- Weight management
- Detoxification and liver cleanse
- Immune support
- Skin health and aging

Website: www.gpnutrition.co.uk
Instagram: GP_NUTRITION
Twitter: GPnutrition

Expert biog 4:
Dr Nigma Talib

Expert biog 5:
Henrietta Norton

Dr. Nigma Talib, a naturopathic doctor, graduated from the Canadian College of Naturopathic Medicine in 2002. Founder and owner of the West Vancouver Wellness Center in British Columbia, where she served on the examination and quality-assurance committees to the College of Naturopathic Physicians of British Columbia, Dr. Talib currently has two naturopathic clinics, one in London and the other in New York. Besides treating chronic illnesses, she works with patients to help them achieve optimal aging from the inside and out with her "non surgical face lift treatments," where she has been linked to Hollywood stars who come to her for regular rejuvenating treatments.

Dr. Talib also regularly delivers presentations at various nutriceutical seminars, educating practitioners of natural medicine throughout the UK, as well as contributing articles on the effective uses of complementary medicine to a range of lifestyle magazines. Dr. Talib has won the Princeton Global Award for being one of the top Naturopathic Doctors in her field.

Areas of specialty

- Naturopathic medicine
- Acupuncture and traditional Chinese medicine
- Botanical medicine
- Homeopathy and functional nutrition
- Bespoke, non-surgical face lift treatments
- Anti-aging and optimal health and wellness

Website: www.healthydoc.com

Henrietta Norton has been working as a nutritional therapist in women's health since 2005. She specializes in fertility and pregnancy and has clinics at the integrated medical practice Grace Belgravia as well as her own clinic in East Sussex. Henrietta is the author of *Take Control of Your Endometriosis*. She is a member of the British Association for Applied Nutrition and Nutritional Therapy (BANT) and the Nutritional Therapy Council (NTC), and associate member of the Royal Society of Medicine (RSM) and the Guild of Health Writers. She is also a Foresight preconception practitioner, an Institute for Functional Medicine (AFMCP) graduate, and is currently completing her MSc in Nutritional Medicine at the University of Surrey.

Henrietta is co-founder of the Food-State supplement brand Wild Nutrition.

In addition, Henrietta is a mother to three young children and so understands the trials and tribulations of fertility, pregnancy, and birth first hand.

Areas of specialty

- Preconception
- Pregnancy
- Female hormonal health
- Detoxification

Website: www.henriettanorton.com

The Knowledge

Like trusted cabbies who study the intricacies of our streets, you should hold the knowledge of how your body works — the back roads, what's causing road blocks to optimal health, and what to do when there is, ahem, traffic build-up in your digestive system. The good news is that all of these solutions can be found in your local farmers' market — or even the supermarket. Replace the pharmacy mentality with frequent trips to the *farm*acy, and your fridge will soon become your new medicine cabinet.

In this section, I aim to give you a good working knowledge of your digestive system so that you can fine tune yours, and walk you through why an alkaline system, or neutral blood pH, can be your body's best state for prevention. And the best tools? Magical, health-giving raw vegetables and fruits flowing with chlorophyll and other super nutrients called phytonutrients.

Becoming familiar with the mechanics of your gut can play such an important role in your immunity, mood, and overall well-being. I talked about my own battle with depression and a streptococcal infection earlier in the book (see page 7), and it was learning about my gut that helped me understand how to utilize my inner physician to problem solve. Think about any time you've had a gut feeling, good or bad. Receive any terrible news? Your first reaction is to feel sick in the stomach. Falling in love? I don't know about you, but those love butterflies have always been in my gut. A healthy gut is your spiritual and emotional navigation, and you must work at keeping it healthy to remain happy and well.

Your Gut Health

A tour of your digestive system

When I started PLENISH, I called on one of my most trusted experts, Romi Pulichino (see page 11), a registered dietitian who came on board to launch the company with me in September 2012. I've asked her to use her no-nonsense approach to paint a simple explanation of the digestive system.

Hunger: feed it, don't kill it

If you ask people why they eat, many answer "Because I'm hungry." Most of us think that the whole purpose of eating is to *kill* hunger. That is an oversimplified version of why we actually find food and put it in our mouths. Leaving aside all socio-anthropological considerations, we are programmed to eat in order to get essential nutrients into our trillions of cells so that they can function properly and keep us alive and well.

Digestion is the process of turning something "macro," like an amazing lunch wrap or a delish smoothie, into microscopic nutrients to feed our cells. For us to be able to actually absorb all of the nutrients from our food into our blood, our digestive system fulfills three main functions:

- liquefies our food
- extracts all the nutrients and water
- eliminates anything we don't need.

1. The brain: where it all begins

Digestion doesn't start when you sit back in your chair and say to the waitress, "Can you please clear my plate, I'm stuffed." The digestion process actually starts in the brain. This command center green-lights the digestion brigade (glands) to get ready. As soon as you visualize your next meal, glands in your mouth and stomach start pumping digestion agents called enzymes. Enzymes are your best friends because, together with teeth and stomach acids, they help you churn all the food that passes through your system.

2. The mouth: chewing it over

The mouth performs a crucial step in digestion. It is the only function in the process over which you have some autonomy and control. You can improve the absorption of nutrients and decrease any kind of indigestion, just by chewing your food thoroughly. After food passes the first phase of breakdown in the mouth, it is moist with saliva and covered with enzymes, so digestion has officially started. It then travels down the esophagus, a tube that connects the mouth to the stomach.

3. The stomach: a bit of kneading

Newsflash: there are NO teeth in the stomach! If you swallow things half-chewed, the only thing your stomach can do is provide some enzymes and gastric acids, and a bit of kneading. Many people experience bloating under the ribcage, as well as acid reflux, after a meal. This can have many causes, but one of the most common ones is that a large amount of partially-chewed food has entered the stomach, especially so in the case of animal products. The best advice is don't rush eating and use those molars to chew like the evolved *homo sapiens* that you are.

4. The small intestine and the liver: in the flow

After visiting your hard-working stomach, partially-digested food travels into the small intestine. This is your very best friend, as it helps complete the last phases of digestion. Both pancreatic and bile juices flow into here, loaded with amazing enzymes for breaking down everything imaginable: carbohydrates, protein, fat, vitamins, and minerals. Finger-like micro cells (or villi) lining the intestinal wall absorb these nutrient molecules into the blood and lymph circulation. Nutrients are then carried to the liver for a final filtering before being poured into the blood and sent off to feed every cell of your body.

5. The colon: kick out the crap — literally!

All debris and undigested material, including dead cells from your intestinal tract, continue on your gut's path to the large intestine or colon, where water is absorbed and fecal matter is formed. If you are a healthy, wholefoods eater, getting rid of this matter will be the highlight of your day. If you eat loads of animal products and processed foods, it might be a painful part of your week. The large intestine is a major detoxification organ. It is crucial to keep it clean and toned so that your precious body can absorb nutrients properly. Think about it — you don't want waste products and toxins sitting inside your body causing you all sorts of health issues. You want that waste out ASAP. Eating a mostly plant-based, wholefoods diet to keep matter flowing through, and being eliminated from, your large intestine, paired with cleansing when your body feels lethargic, will help you maintain a healthy and young digestive system. In turn, that will translate to a healthy mind and a healthy body.

Healthy gut, no more rut

Next time someone tells you that what you're feeling is "all in your head," correct them and say that mental fog and lethargy can be due to gut congestion. Feeling low on mental stamina? Start by evaluating your eating and pooping habits. The gastrointestinal system is known as the second brain because its walls contain over 100 million neurons (more than the spinal cord), it works with over 30 neurotransmitters and produces over 90 percent of the feel-good serotonin in your body. When your small and large intestine (colon) are not properly absorbing nutrients and regularly disposing of debris (pooping), inflammation and damage to the tissue occur and your second brain cannot perform at full capacity.

A high-fiber diet full of antioxidant-rich fruits and vegetables will tone your system from the inside

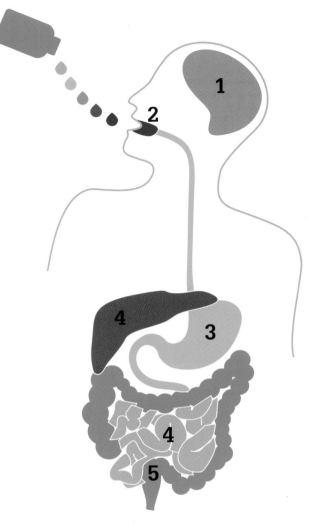

out, helping you to keep nasty toxins at bay and repair damage to cell tissue from free radicals.

When you feel low on life mojo, ask yourself: "Am I constipated? Have I been eating crap?" If so, you may benefit from cutting out dairy, animal products, and processed food, and juicing or cleansing your way back to feeling good.

Get pHabulous!

All about alkalinity

Now that you are familiar with how the body processes your food, let's delve into which foods you should choose to fuel your body's cells and how those choices affect your overall health.

Establishing a peaceful state

Blood pH is a measure of how alkaline or acidic your system is. This is determined by how acidic or alkaline the foods you eat are (combined with other factors, such as stress). If you have a low pH, this means you are acidic (see pages 18–19). This can adversely affect your health at the cellular level, making you susceptible to fatigue, osteoporosis, candida, loss of muscle, kidney stones, and, most dramatically, an increase in free radicals — which can damage cells and is one of the many contributors in developing cancer.

Think of your blood pH as any other environment, domestic or political. Bad things usually happen under bad circumstances. You want to create a happy society, with contented, peaceful citizens (cells) and no free "radicals" wreaking havoc.

Your body works very hard to stay in an alkaline state — also known as homeostasis. If you are too acidic, your body will start robbing alkaline minerals from places that need them, like your pearly white teeth, bones, and bodily tissues.

The best way to prevent a nasty list of "dis-eases" is to get your blood/ body systems in an alkaline state.

Relax, you're not being hunted

When we are stressed, our bodies release the acid-forming hormones adrenaline and cortisol. Take a trip down memory lane to science class where you learned about the fight or flight syndrome — the reaction of an animal being hunted by a predator. Cortisol and adrenaline levels soar, preparing the animal to flee from the predator or fight for its life. Granted, most of us don't live in daily fear of a life-threatening predator, but the same chemical reaction happens when your boss pulls you up on a below-par performance, the stock you are long on takes a massive dip, or you are trying to beat the clock. This chemical reaction affects our pH.

The best ways to get alkaline

The good news is that eating and drinking alkaline foods and juices is the easiest, most efficient way to PLENISH your cells with alkaline minerals, keeping you on the path of optimum well-being. The mind–body connection is just as powerful, so make sure you work on your mind to complement the changes you are making to your diet.

Unwind your mind

Finding ways to unwind at the end of your day, like taking exercise, connecting with someone you love, or engaging in five minutes of meditation, can have a huge impact on lowering your cortisol levels.

Target your body

You can shift your pH levels by adding lots of alkaline plant foods to your diet, and reducing the amount of acid-forming processed foods and animal products in your diet. Notice I said reduce, not eliminate, as it's all about balance. Some alkaline and acid-forming foods are listed below and shown on the chart overleaf.

Acid Foods made from and containing cows' milk; prescription drugs; artificial sweeteners; processed foods like pastries, breads, and gluten pasta; animal proteins like meat, fish, dairy products, and protein powders; most starchy vegetables and grains.

Alkaline Most vegetables, particularly non-starchy greens like lettuce, spinach, kale, and collard greens; fresh fruits; some grains such as quinoa, amaranth, millet, and teff.

Acidic ➔ Alkaline

3　4　5　6　7　8　9　10

What does alkaline mean?

Alkalinity is a measure of pH levels.

- Above 7: you're in alkaline territory
- At 7: you're at a neutral blood pH
- Below 7: the more acidic you are, the less oxygen your blood has, so not a good result

You can test your pH at home using litmus paper, but I recommend having it done by a nutritional therapist or doctor, as your pH levels vary greatly during a normal day and results can therefore be misleading. The effects of what you've eaten that day will not have an immediate effect on your test (for example, if you chug a green juice after a pizza binge, you won't see a spike and then a drop in pH). This is convincing proof that consistently eating mainly alkaline foods is the way to keep your system pHabulously alkaline.

Expert tip

Chlorophyll, found in green vegetables (see pages 20–21) is a powerful phytochemical that has a very alkalizing effect on the body, so if you are eating anything acidic, such as fish or eggs, make sure you have a large portion of these veggies, or an alkalizing green veg juice, on the side.

Chlorophyll

Liquid sunshine

To talk about chlorophyll, we need to talk about photosynthesis. First, let's brush up on what photosynthesis is.

noun: photosynthesis. The process by which green plants use sunlight to synthesize nutrients from carbon dioxide and water. Photosynthesis in plants generally involves the green pigment chlorophyll and generates oxygen as a by-product.

Chlorophyll is the magical phytochemical that gives plants their green color. Via photosynthesis, chlorophyll takes the Sun's energy and converts it into carbohydrates — it is both responsible and necessary for life on earth. Major!

When we eat green plants, we indirectly get our energy from the Sun, hence why we call chlorophyll liquid sunshine.

Chlorophyll shalt give oxygen

In addition to providing energy, the molecular structure of chlorophyll is nearly identical to our own hemoglobin, the oxygen carrier in human blood, and serves a similar oxygen-delivering purpose in humans as it does in plants. The bottom line is chlorophyll improves the transport of oxygen to your cells, and in turn gives you more energy.

Thou shalt cleanse

Chlorophyll is also very cleansing, helping to remove toxins from our blood that come from the food we eat and the air we breathe.

A study in *The Journal of Toxicological Sciences* in Japan (see the Bibliography on page 143) found that mice that were given chlorophyll eliminated more toxic substances (specifically mercury) than a control group. These findings suggest that the mercury-binding properties of chlorophyll also work in humans.

Juicing your green vegetables is a great way to maximize chlorophyll intake. The juicer breaks down chlorophyll's cell walls, releasing the valuable nutrients within, so that your body cells can absorb them instantly.

In the raw

The power of living foods

I have a lot of friends (and clients) who are very intimidated by the term "raw foods," thinking that it involves some radical and complicated regime that only yoga-mat-toting, green-juice-drinking people would follow. The irony is, raw food is the most simple way of eating: no cooking; no intricate sauces; minimal dish washing. It simply means eating plant-based foods in their most natural state (uncooked) and whole food that has not been heated above 104–113°F, chemically preserved, or refined. What's hippie dippy about that?

A life-giving force

Plant-based foods like fresh fruits and vegetables are literally life giving. They contain vitamins, minerals, phytochemicals, and enzymes that bring oxygen and nourishment to your cells, and help your body flush out the toxins that it consumes. But when you cook them (above 108°F), these foods lose their life-giving force and don't have the same healing power as in their uncooked state.

Raw ambition

It's not that cooked foods are bad, but if you want to give yourself the best opportunity to ward off disease and feel and look at your peak it's worth reviewing the proportion of raw foods versus cooked foods that you consume. The ultimate goal is 80 percent raw, 20 percent cooked (see plate A). If you're just getting started, try 60 percent raw, 40 percent cooked (see plate B) and work your way up.

That said, everyone's nutritional needs are different, and there are no rigid rules about the correct percentage. Experiment between 60 and 80 percent raw to find out what makes you feel your absolute best, then that's your perfect proportion.

Juice yourself raw

When you think that over 4lb of raw produce can go into a single juice, it's easy to see how a fresh juice can swing your proportions of raw to cooked foods in favor of raw. Juicing is an easy, convenient way to increase your raw intake. By eating a large proportion of your daily intake in its raw form, you maintain the vitamins, minerals, phytochemicals, and live-giving force that will PLENISH your body at a deep level.

A

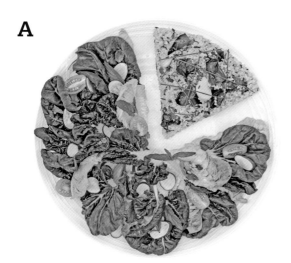

B

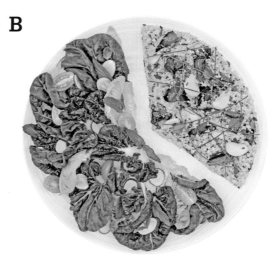

Phytonutrients

The power base of plants

Phytonutrients (sometimes called phytochemicals) are nutritious little compounds produced by plants to protect them from their own health threats — bacteria and viruses. When you eat plants, your body benefits from the protective phytonutrients that you ingest.

Eat a rainbow

Phytonutrients give vegetables and fruits their beautiful bright colors, such as an orange carrot, a red pepper, or a purple cabbage.

Recent studies have shown that eating large amounts of brightly colored fruits and vegetables, nuts, wholegrains, and beans containing phytochemicals guards your cells against damage from free radicals. They may also decrease the risk of developing certain cancers, as well as heart disease and hypertension.

There are thousands and thousands of phytonutrients, and only some of them have well-researched health benefits. Unlike vitamins and minerals, there is no RDA (recommended daily allowance) of phytonutrients, so eat a rainbow of brightly colored vegetables and fruits to make sure you are getting the optimum amount of phytonutrient superpower in your diet.

Sugar

You are sweet enough

Sugar has emerged in the media as a major villain in the war against diabetes, obesity, and cancer. It's easy to get confused about which sugars are healthy and which you should avoid. Luckily for us, nutritional therapist Gabriela Peacock (see page 12) has outlined the basics we all need to know about what we should and shouldn't be including in our diet.

A tale of two carbs

Carbohydrates are classified into two basic groups:

Complex carbohydrates, or starches, are composed of many simple sugars joined together by chemical bonds. The more bonds, the more complex a carbohydrate; the more complex a carbohydrate, the more slowly it is broken down. Complex carbohydrates are recommended due to their slow release of sugar into the bloodstream and, consequently, for sustained energy levels.

Simple carbohydrates are either monosaccharides (one-sugar molecules) or disaccharides (two-sugar molecules). The principal monosaccharides that occur in foods are glucose and fructose, and the major disaccharides are sucrose (white cane sugar) and lactose (found in milk).

How sugar is used in the body

Glucose is the primary source of energy required for every cell to function, and it's also the primary unit that makes up complex starches. When we talk about blood sugar, we are referring to glucose in the blood. When we eat carbohydrates, our body breaks them down into glucose. When blood glucose levels rise, cells in the pancreas release insulin, signaling the cells to take up glucose from the blood. As the cells absorb blood sugar, glucose levels start to drop.

Fruit sugars versus refined sugars

Fructose (fruit sugar) is a simple, naturally occurring sugar found in plants. It is very sweet, roughly one and a half times sweeter than sucrose (see below). The food industry processes naturally occurring fructose to make a refined, super-sweet (and super-scary) version called high-fructose corn syrup (HFCS). The worldwide increase in the consumption of sweeteners, soft drinks, and foods containing HFCS means fructose intake has rapidly increased. Don't confuse fructose found naturally in fruit and vegetables with fructose in HFCS or other sweeteners.

Sucrose is the refined, crystallized, white sugar found in many households and processed foodstuffs. It consists of 50 percent glucose and 50 percent fructose and is broken down into its constituent parts in the small intestine, resulting in immediate elevations in blood sugar levels. Because of its glucose content, sucrose has a high-GI value of 65. By comparison, naturally occurring fructose has no impact on insulin production, does not raise blood sugar, and has a lower GI than in

processed foods. It has been used by diabetics, as it's thought to aid glycemic control.

Low-GI fruits and vegetables with naturally occurring fructose are beneficial for keeping you feeling full and energized, and encouraging the body to burn fat. We always recommend mixing super-low GI vegetables with fruit juices to keep the overall sugar content to a minimum, while getting all of the goodness (enzymes, phytonutrients, vitamins, and minerals) from the fruits and vegetables.

GI explained

The glycemic index (GI) is a ranking of carbohydrates (sugar) on a scale of 0 (low) to 100 (high) for how quickly foods make your blood sugar levels rise after eating them. High-GI foods are very easily broken down and so rapidly increase blood sugar levels. Your insulin response mechanism keeps your blood sugar balanced, but it can become challenged over time if you are constantly consuming too many high-GI foods (a main factor contributing to diabetes, obesity and other chronic illnesses). Your best bet for optimal health and energy management is to stick to mostly low-GI fruits and vegetables. High-GI foods tend to be refined, simple sugars and low-GI foods tend to be unrefined, complex carbs.

The GI of foods is affected by cooking storing, and processing. A raw vegetable or fruit tends to have an even lower GI than its cooked counterpart.

The lowest of the low are the best of the best

Fruits and veg with the lowest GI include:

Apples and pears | Grapefruit, lemons, and limes | Stone fruits, e.g. cherries, peaches, and plums | Raspberries and blueberries | Rhubarb | Carrots | Leafy greens

Fruits with a moderate GI include:

Pineapple | Mangos | Papaya | Kiwi fruit | Bananas | Watermelon

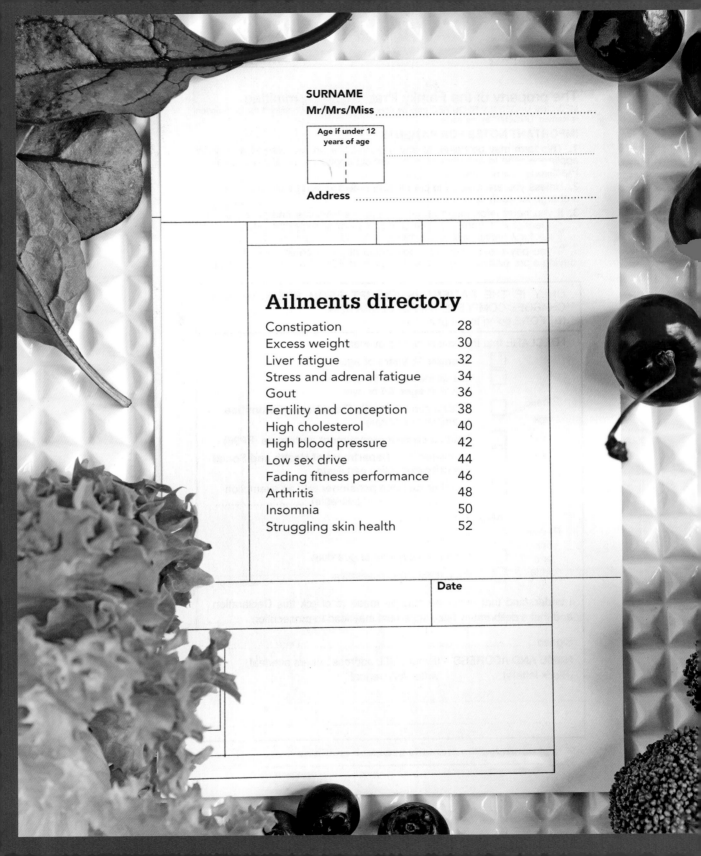

SURNAME
Mr/Mrs/Miss ....

Age if under 12
years of age

Address ....

Ailments directory

Constipation   28
Excess weight   30
Liver fatigue   32
Stress and adrenal fatigue   34
Gout   36
Fertility and conception   38
High cholesterol   40
High blood pressure   42
Low sex drive   44
Fading fitness performance   46
Arthritis   48
Insomnia   50
Struggling skin health   52

Date

What's Ailing You?

Are you thriving or surviving?

I was surviving not thriving with a mean case of strep throat and depression due to a gut that was completely out of whack. So what's your issue? Gout? Low sex drive? Constantly constipated, or can't stop craving sugar? At PLENISH, we meet lots of clients from all walks of life who have one thing in common: they know they want to use a juice cleanse to hit CTRL + ALT + DELETE on their health to get them back to fighting form. The selection of ailments featured here is based on the conditions we most commonly encounter in our clientele, in the hope that we can help you tackle what's ailing you. I've broken out the big guns from my little green book of experts (see pages 10–13) to get to the root of these common conditions.

Treating illness is expensive, so why not commit to spending more on wellness than on sickness and see how it prioritizes your spending. Shelling out buckets a day on coffee? Replace that with spending next to nothing on green tea and you can afford to buy organic, or skip a night out on the booze once a week for two months and buy a juicer (see page 56)!

How to use the key

Each ailment in this chapter comes with its very own icon and juice menu. Look for the icon relevant to your ailment in the Juice Recipes chapter (pages 60–107). These will be the recipes featured in the juice menus.

 Constipation

 Excess weight

 Liver fatigue

 Stress and adrenal fatigue

 Gout

 Fertility and conception

 High cholesterol

 High blood pressure

 Low sex drive

 Fading fitness performance

 Arthritis

 Insomnia

 Struggling skin health

Remember, all juices in this book are tried-and-tested delicious so worth drinking up, ailment or not.

Constipation

Poop. Poop. Poop. We said it, we said it again, and we'll keep saying it until you stop squirming! All humans need to take in vital nutrients to keep their metabolic functions running, and eliminate (poop/pee/sweat) the toxins and bits we don't need. When this very basic function slows down, it can wreak havoc on our system. I asked Gabriela Peacock (see page 12) to take us through how to keep digestive traffic moving smoothly and what to do when your inner transport system goes on strike.

What is constipation?

Constipation is a common condition that can affect people of all ages. During digestion (see pages 15–16), food is broken down and most of the nutrients get absorbed into the bloodstream via a vein called the hepatic portal vein. This vein travels directly to the liver. Fiber is undigested and so remains in the bowel, adding bulk to the waste products and making it easer for poop to be pushed along the length of the large intestine by muscular contractions called peristalsis. Once the excess water has been absorbed, the solid waste is temporarily stored in the rectum before elimination. But with constipation, the waste remains in the intestines for a much longer period of time, and consequently some of the toxins get reabsorbed back into the bloodstream, burdening the liver. Constipation can also worsen the hormone imbalance in women, leading to estrogen dominance. Women are supposed to break down large quantities of estrogen each day in their liver and excrete it through bowel motions. Constipated women reabsorb much of that estrogen as it recirculates back to the liver.

Do you have it?

Symptoms include less frequent than normal bowel movements, straining to make them, and difficulty emptying the bowel completely. During constipation, poop is often hard, dry, or lumpy and may be accompanied by wind, bloating, and abdominal pain. Symptoms of hormone imbalance as a consequence of constipation can include premenstrual syndrome (PMS) and menstrual cramps. Constipation can be short term, causing no lasting problems, but chronic constipation can be painful and lead to complications such as hemorrhoids and incontinence. Diagnosis is normally made on the basis of symptoms, but tests may be taken to rule out more serious problems.

What's causing it?

The most common causes of constipation include too little fiber in the diet, insufficient fluid, changes to the daily routine, and lack of exercise. It can also be a side effect of stress, some medications, and associated health conditions, such as irritable bowel syndrome (IBS). A sedentary (i.e. too much sofa slumping) lifestyle can exacerbate constipation, as can changes to the diet as a consequence of long-distance travel and pregnancy.

Let's get it sorted!

Dietary changes that increase fiber and fluid intake can alleviate constipation by adding bulk to the poop. This increases the frequency of bowel movements and reduces the amount of time between consumption of a food and its elimination from the body.

Warning

Report any change in bowel habits to your doctor, particularly if there is blood or mucus in your poop. If you've recently consumed beet juice, your poop and urine may turn red, so don't be alarmed!

Up your fiber

Consumption of whole fruits and vegetables adds soluble and insoluble fiber to the diet, which can help push accumulated waste through the colon. It is recommended that adults consume 18–30g of fiber each day to keep "regular." During juicing, insoluble plant fibers, which slow digestion, are separated from the nutrient-dense, hydrating liquid. The result is a juice full of active enzymes, energizing and easily metabolized natural sugars, oxygen, and an abundance of vitamins, minerals, and phytonutrients that are easily absorbed to support a healthy digestive system and liver function, ensuring that you are not holding on to waste and reabsorbing toxins into the bloodstream that your body has worked so hard to eliminate. Eating oats, bran, and wholegrains will also help increase your fiber intake.

Get drinking and moving

Make sure you drink at least 6–8 glasses of water per day. Herbal teas containing fennel, peppermint, or nettle are also recommended. And be sure to exercise for at least 20 minutes a day.

Drink freshly pressed juice on an empty stomach. This increases the absorption of nutrients into the bloodstream of the small intestine. The blood then circulates throughout the body, offering the vital organs a power shot of readily assimilated nutrients. It also works to alkalize the blood (see pages 17–19) and helps hydrate the small and large intestine for optimal waste removal.

The FARMacy

These are Gabriela's recommended fruits and vegetables for keeping things moving smoothly:

Papaya juice is rich in the protein-digesting (proteolytic) enzyme papain and so helps break down dietary proteins in the stomach and intestines. Papaya helps regulate the digestive system, supports peristalsis (see "What is constipation" opposite) and promotes regular bowel movements. People who experience irritation along the gastrointestinal tract, especially relating to excessive wind or a tendency toward constipation, have reported benefits from including papaya in their diet.

Apples contain sorbitol (also known as glucitol), which acts as a natural laxative. It is a type of sugar alcohol that is slowly absorbed into the bloodstream. Sorbitol holds on to some water as it makes its way through the gut, drawing it into the large intestine. This increases the moisture content of the poop (done squirming now?), making it looser, and promoting regular bowel movements. Sorbitol is also found in prunes, peaches, and pears.

Carrot juice helps to support the liver — which produces bile, a lack of which can contribute to constipation — by binding with the bile acids, encouraging peristalsis and the movement of waste through the intestine. Juiced carrots taste sweet but their sugar and calorie content is much lower than that of the fruit. Unless you want a perma-tan, don't drink too much. The phytonutrient beta-carotene can turn your skin orange if eaten in excess.

Juice menu

Page 93: Smooth Move

Superfood Booster

Flax seeds (linseeds) and **psyllium husks** are rich in soluble fiber and psyllium helps support regular bowel movements. Stir powdered psyllium husks into a juice to cleanse the colon and relieve constipation.

Prunes can help by encouraging softer, more easily passed poop. Soak overnight in cold water, then strain and drink the natural sweet juice left behind.

Excess Weight

At PLENISH, we don't promote juice cleanses for weight loss, but many of our clients do cleanse to drop a few pesky pounds, or to jumpstart a weight-loss program. You will lose weight on a juice cleanse, if done properly, but to lose weight safely, and long term, the changes you make post-cleanse are just as important (see page 120). Losing weight takes discipline. A juice cleanse is a great way to break bad habits and build confidence in your own self-control. Clients typically feel so great after a cleanse that they are motivated to keep up healthy eating habits to sustain the feeling. I've asked Gabriela Peacock (see page 12), a nutritional therapist and ex-model (who knows a thing or two about keeping slim), to deliver the hard science behind weight loss and keeping cravings at bay.

What's causing it?

Overeating and under-exercising are almost always the causes of excess weight. In other words, the energy balance is skewed. Consuming more calories than are used up results in excess energy being stored as fat. Diets high in sugar, and those based around processed, refined foods, tend to cause more weight gain than those that include plenty of fruits and vegetables, healthy proteins, good fats, and wholegrain carbohydrates.

There is a lot of confusing information about carbs, protein, and fat in the media, so here is a recap on how these "macronutrients" are used in the body, so that you can create an eating plan that works for you.

Carbohydrate is used for energy. If too much is eaten, some will be stored as glycogen, the storage form of glucose, in muscle and liver.

Protein is broken down into its component peptides and amino acids and used to replace protein lost by routine cell turnover in muscles, and also to make enzymes and other key chemicals needed for metabolism.

Fats are primarily used for energy. Only a small amount replaces the fat lost in cell membranes and the nervous system. The rate at which fat is oxidized to produce energy does not vary much. If more fat is consumed than can be used, the rest of the fat is stored.

Let's get it sorted!

Balance your sugar levels

Persistent blood sugar imbalance is often linked to weight-management problems. The overconsumption of simple sugars that the body doesn't use for energy turns to fat. Excess sugar can also cause imbalances in the nervous system, nutritional deficiencies, and fluctuating hormone levels.

After eating, sugar is released into the bloodstream. In response, the pancreas secretes the hormone insulin to keep the level of blood sugar within a safe range. Eating simple, refined sugars (from food products like white bread and candies) causes a rapid, temporary spike in insulin that is followed by a "low" that leaves us feeling much worse. It is important for optimal health that the blood sugar levels and insulin production are balanced, and one of the best ways to do this is to choose whole, complex, unrefined foods including plenty of fruits, vegetables, protein, and good sources of fat. See The PLENISH Pantry Makeover on page 114.

Beat your cravings

Blood sugar imbalance is also thought to play a major role in the development of cravings. Throughout the day, blood glucose levels can fluctuate, meaning that they lie outside of ideal levels and can cause cravings, irritability, and mood swings. Emotional factors may result in you turning to food for comfort. Getting to grips with what, when, and why you are eating can help you to identify triggers that can be adjusted to create a healthier, more balanced diet. Additionally, if we go too long without eating and blood sugar falls, it can result in food cravings and overeating. Adding a fresh juice as a snack could also help to increase the efficiency of your metabolism, particularly if you try our recommended recipe (see Juice menu below).

Turn to drink

It is important to remain hydrated, as dehydration can make you feel hungry when you are in fact thirsty. Drink at least 6–8 glasses of water a day.

Get exercising

Exercise reduces stress hormones such as cortisol and increases mood-boosting ones such as endorphins. Endorphins are chemicals in the body that help us to feel good, and are released into the bloodstream along with the other happy hormones serotonin, dopamine, and adrenaline when we exercise. Move it for at least 30 minutes a day.

Feel full on fewer calories

Add green tea to a juice or smoothie. It's a rich source of phytonutrients called catechins, which can increase the hormone responsible for making you feel full. Psyllium husks, which are high in fiber and low in calories, help improve digestion and are also known to increase that satisfied feeling, encouraging you to eat less later. They expand when mixed with liquid, so soak overnight in a juice or water.

The FARMacy

These are Gabriela's recommended fruits and vegetables for keeping cravings under control:

Broccoli contains chromium, a key constitute of glucose tolerance factor — a compound that acts with insulin to support the cellular uptake of glucose. Glucose tolerance factor helps to drive blood sugar into the cells more quickly after eating. Chromium has also been shown to help control food cravings and reduce appetite. Broccoli is

an ideal vegetable to add to a juice, as it's low in calories and sugar.

Grapefruit is known to stimulate the metabolism. It is low in calories and high in vitamin C, which helps absorb chromium. Grapefruits are rich in flavonoids, and one specific phytochemical in grapefruit called monoterpene is an effective appetite suppressant. It also improves digestion and stimulates liver and gall bladder function to support the breakdown of fat.

Avocados can't be juiced but are great for creamy smoothies or shakes. While they are relatively high in calories, more than two-thirds of those calories come from the monounsaturated fat oleic acid. Studies have demonstrated that monounsaturated fats like oleic acid are much more likely to be used by your body as a slow-burning energy source, keeping blood sugar levels balanced.

Juice menu

Page 89: Craving Killa'

Superfood Booster

Cayenne pepper is rich in capsaicinoids, phytonutrients known to support thermogenesis — the process of heat production within the body — which is a contributor to energy production and metabolic rate that influence weight management.

Cinnamon decreases blood sugar levels and enhances the action of insulin, so is great for diabetics or anyone who experiences regular sugar cravings. Sprinkle on foods or add to smoothies to keep your blood sugar evenly regulated.

Spirulina provides an abundant supply of phytonutrients that boost our health. It is a rich source of protein, vital for the growth and repair of tissues, and plays a significant part in balancing blood sugar. Add a heaping teaspoon to a juice or smoothie to kickstart the day.

🍷 Liver Fatigue

One of the most common fears we encounter with clients who come to PLENISH is, "I think I did some serious damage to my liver last night/ week/year." Whether you've been consuming too much booze or eating processed foods on the go, your inner physician can often tell you when your liver needs a little TLC. I've asked Gabriela Peacock (see page 12) to shed some light on what your precious liver is meant to do, and what actually happens when said liver is asked to work at 110 percent all of the time.

What is liver fatigue?

As the body's largest internal organ, the liver plays a crucial role in metabolism. Perhaps its most prominent role is detoxification — acting as a filter to deactivate and eliminate toxins from the blood. Without an efficient liver and healthy kidneys, toxins and waste products remain in the blood.

Do you have it?

Liver fatigue can lead to symptoms of poor circulation, digestive problems, headaches, skin-related allergies, hormonal imbalances, and, if overburdened for long enough, death (we're talking in extreme cases here).

What's causing it?

Every day, the liver manufactures and secretes approximately 2 pints of bile. Bile is necessary for the absorption of fat-soluble material from the intestines, including many vitamins, and its secretion helps eliminate many toxic substances. Many factors determine whether the liver performs its critical functions well.

We are exposed to thousands of toxins on a daily basis (from the air, smoking, alcohol, medications, stress, house-cleaning products, and cosmetics) as well as chemicals (from pesticides, hormones in foods, additives — such as colorings, flavorings, and preservatives — genetically engineered foods, and unclean drinking water). The liver deactivates these substances and sends them to be excreted by the bowels (yep, more poop), lungs, kidneys, or skin.

Excess pressure on the liver from overeating, eating overly rich or poor-quality food, environmental stresses, overwork, or emotional stress can cause liver overload, leading to a decreased ability to clear toxins and hormones and manufacture bile. An overloaded liver allows toxic waste material to pass into the blood and the body.

Let's get it sorted!

Detoxify

Liver detoxification is a complex two-phase process that involves a series of reactions. Both phases require specific essential nutrients like B vitamins, folic acid, and sulfur, and antioxidants such as beta-carotene, vitamins E and C, and selenium. Through this detoxification process, toxins are converted into water-soluble molecules that can then be excreted through the colon, kidneys, or skin. With the constant demand on the liver, it is important to support it by providing all the nutrients it needs. Bowel function is also important for the elimination of toxins (see pages 28–29).

Eat your greens

Foods that can help with both phases of detoxification include cruciferous vegetables such as kale, cabbage, broccoli, and Brussels sprouts. Dark green vegetables are bursting with chlorophyll (see pages 20–21), which can neutralize harmful chemicals. Naturally cleansing bitter and astringent greens like nettles, watercress, arugula, dandelion, and mustard greens can help purify tissues.

Seek sweet protection

Antioxidant-rich fruits (berries, citrus fruits, and apples) help protect the liver from cell damage caused by high levels of free radicals that are naturally produced during detoxification.

The FARMacy

Gabriela recommends the following fruits and vegetables to help support liver function:

Brightly colored fruits and vegetables are all packed with antioxidants needed for liver detoxification and protecting liver cells.

Beet has long been used for medicinal purposes, primarily for disorders of the liver, given their stimulating effects on the liver's detoxification processes. The phytonutrient pigment that gives it its rich purple color, betacyanin, supports phase-two detoxification, the bile duct and gall bladder, as well as the regeneration of liver cells. Beet also helps purify the blood and is capable of absorbing heavy metals, thereby reducing the toxic load on the liver.

Lemon juice contains citric acid, which acts as a stimulant to the digestive system and a cleansing agent for the intestines (lemon is a natural antiseptic that kills harmful bacteria). Lemon juice is also a great detoxifier, contributing to the body's alkalinity (see page 17), and supports liver function by strengthening liver enzymes.

Kale is a leafy green member of the cruciferous family, containing sulfurous compounds called sulforaphane and indole 3 carbinol (I3C) that support liver detoxification. It's also bursting with chlorophyll and carotenes that aid the detoxification pathway. It contains glucosinolates, which help the liver to produce natural enzymes required to remove carcinogens, thereby lowering the risks associated with cancer.

Juice menu

Page 97: Liver Supporter

Superfood Booster

Turmeric can help fight infections, reduce inflammation, and aid digestion. It contains a high concentration of the phytonutrient pigment curcumin, a potent antioxidant that protects the liver. It stimulates bile production and excretion via the gall bladder, improving the body's ability to digest fats. Add a teaspoon of ground turmeric to your juice or to foods when cooking.

Stress and Adrenal Fatigue

Ever think that stress is just a state of mind? Think again. The physiological effects of stress are as real as taxes. "Adrenal fatigue" is a relatively new buzz-worthy term that describes a host of symptoms (including fatigue, dark circles, trouble sleeping) that indicate your overachieving schedule or life issues are more than you can physically cope with. Before embarking on my journey to the juice (see pages 6–9), a lot of my symptoms were largely due to being adrenally fatigued without even knowing what that meant at the time. Educate your inner physician so that when you start to feel adrenally fatigued, you can nip it in the bud. Here, Gabriela Peacock (see page 12) looks at the effects on the body when the mind–body connection is too tightly bound for comfort, and how to remedy and prevent it.

What is adrenal fatigue?

Stress triggers a set of biological responses: the release of the stress hormones adrenaline and cortisol from the adrenal glands (small glands that sit on top of your kidneys); an increase in blood sugar; flexing of the muscles; shallow breathing; rising blood pressure and rapid heart rate. All these responses are designed to help meet physical challenges that threaten survival — known as fight or flight (see page 17). The trouble is that most modern-day stresses are not resolved by action. Instead, we just sit there and seethe while our stress responses are on full alert, to the point of exhaustion. Over time, the adrenal glands become overworked and, in reaction to the stress levels, have difficulty producing these hormones in the right amount. This is known as adrenal fatigue.

What are the long-term effects?

Prolonged activation of the fight or flight response can be linked to a myriad of other related conditions. Elevated adrenaline and cortisol levels trigger the release of excess testosterone. This can drive the body toward insulin resistance (a precursor to diabetes), weight gain (particularly around the middle area of the body), and have a direct inhibitory effect on the reproductive system. Long-term stress can also affect the digestive processes and inhibit the absorption of nutrients. It may also impair the immune system, increasing

your susceptibility to illness. A continued state of stress can suppress serotonin, which in turn may increase anxiety and appetite and can trigger mood disorders such as depression. Research suggests that prolonged chronic stress can be one of the major risk factors in the development of heart disease and diabetes. Elevated levels of the amino acid homocysteine, which often correspond with high levels of cortisol circulating the body, have been identified as a risk factor for cardiovascular disease (see pages 40–41).

Let's get it sorted!

Good news! Through diet and lifestyle changes you can make significant steps on the road to recovery.

Head to bed

The first step in dealing with adrenal fatigue is to get some good-quality sleep. This is when the body is able to repair and regenerate, and it's also a time when we allow the stress hormones to naturally fall. Aiming for eight hours uninterrupted sleep is the ideal, and the sleep you have before midnight is generally better quality.

Eat regularly

Never skip meals and, because blood cortisol levels work closely with blood sugar levels, it's important to avoid snacks containing refined carbohydrates and sugars that will spike blood sugar levels. Instead, opt for complex carbohydrates found in gluten-free grains, such as buckwheat or quinoa, and vegetables, and combine protein with carbohydrate in every meal for a steadier release of glucose into the blood. Stimulants, such as caffeine and alcohol, should also be removed or significantly reduced and replaced with plenty of nutrient-dense fuel such as green juices (see pages 62–77).

Resolve the underlying issue

Probably the most important step is to address the underlying cause of the stress and adrenal fatigue, and where possible remove this trigger. If it's a work-related issue, then figuring out what can be done to improve the situation is going to be the first part of the journey for you.

Learn the art of relaxation

Relaxation techniques, such as yoga, meditation, and tai chi, can offer many stress-busting benefits.

The FARMacy

Gabriela recommends the following fruits and vegetables for combating adrenal fatigue:

Superfood Booster

Maca is a root vegetable rich in calcium, phosphorus, magnesium, potassium, some B vitamins, and iron. Working as an adaptogen — aiding the body's natural ability to adapt to stress — maca is reputed to bring our bodies into balance, and to increase strength and endurance in helping to manage stress.

Juice menu
Page 85: Stress Buster

Beet greens are very nutritious, and worth adding to a juice for their low-fat and antioxidant properties. As with the roots, the green, leafy tops are a good source of the phytochemical compound betaine, which has homocysteine-lowering properties in the blood (see pages 40–41). All green leafy vegetables are valuable in stress-busting juices for their high magnesium content. Chronic stress depletes the body of magnesium, which is important for relaxation and reducing homocysteine levels.

Kiwi fruit is rich in the antioxidant vitamins C and E, flavonoids, anthocyanins, and carotenoids. They also contain a relatively high level of serotonin — an important neurotransmitter (brain chemical) responsible for a number of physiological functions including mood regulation and sleep patterns. Serotonin has a calming effect on most individuals.

Oranges are rich in vitamin C, but they also contain a high level of magnesium and potassium. Vitamin C has been proven to naturally lower cortisol levels.

Celery contains phytonutrients called phthalides, found to have a sedative effect, so if you are feeling stressed and can't sleep, put a stick in it. Phthalides have also been shown to reduce stress hormones and work to relax the muscle walls in arteries, increasing blood flow. As a result, it has long been used in Chinese medicine to help control high blood pressure. Celery is also a very good source source of vitamins K and C, potassium, folate, dietary fiber, molybdenum, manganese, and vitamin B6.

👣 Gout

Since starting PLENISH, we've spoken to hundreds of cleanse clients (usually men) who are young sufferers of gout. Their stories are pretty similar — they work hard, play hard, and often have a diet rich in decadent, acidic foods like meat and in alcohol. We've had really great responses from our gout sufferers who have undergone a juice cleanse, then worked with our nutritional therapist Eve Kalinik (see page 12) to adjust their diet toward a more alkaline state. Seeing the amazing progress they've made under her care, I asked Eve to give you the lowdown on how she has treated our clients, and how to relieve yourself of excess uric acid to gain a gout-free existence.

What is gout?

Gout is a very common disorder caused by a build-up of uric acid in the blood. Uric acid is a waste product made in the body every day that should be efficiently excreted via the kidneys. If your system is overproducing uric acid or under-excreting it (i.e. not peeing it out), that can lead to a depositing of monosodium urate crystals in your body's soft tissues, such as joints, tendons, kidneys, and in other internal tissues, leading to the rapid onset of pain, inflammation, and damage.

Do you have it?

Symptoms typically include inflamed painful joints in the extremities such as the hands, feet, ankles, and wrists. The skin in these affected areas tends to turn red, shiny, and swollen. Blood tests can be used as a way to check serum uric acid levels but are not always a dependable way to make a complete diagnosis. If left untreated, gout can cause joint destruction, and renal damage may occur if the crystals are deposited in the kidneys.

What's causing it?

Possible causes of gout include excess alcohol intake, excessive oxidative stress, a predisposition to it (thanks, Dad!), and metabolic disorders (a medical term for the triple threat of diabetes, high blood pressure, and obesity). It may also be due to an overproduction of uric acid from an overconsumption of foods high in purines. What are purines you may ask? Uric acid is the final breakdown product of purine metabolism. Foods high in purine content include beef, sardines, and variety meats, such as liver, mussels, and anchovies.

Let's get it sorted!

Neutralize

A key part of reducing symptoms is to increase uric acid solubility through a more alkaline pH in the body (see page 17), which will help to neutralize the acid. This means increasing alkaline foods such as leafy greens and natural diuretics like lettuce, cherries, and beets (see opposite).

Calm and cleanse

It's also important to exclude or minimize certain inflammatory food groups from your diet, which includes refined carbohydrates, saturated fats, and alcohol. Cleansing and adding raw vegetable juices to your diet can therefore be very beneficial.

The FARMacy

These are Eve's recommended fruits and vegetables for getting gout before it gets you:

Cherries are one of the hero anti-gout foods to call out, as they help to block the reabsorption of uric acid and increase its excretion. Cherries are also believed to block xanthine oxidase, the enzyme responsible for producing uric acid, thereby reducing production of uric acid itself. And further to this, they contain antioxidant anthocyanins, which may have anti-inflammatory benefits.

Beet, celery, and lettuces such as romaine are all natural diuretics, stimulating urination and the excretion of uric acid. Beet also contain a unique source of the phytonutrient betacyanin, which provides antioxidant, anti-inflammatory, and detoxification support. Lettuce and other leafy vegetables such as kale are excellent sources of folic acid, which has a similar uric acid enzyme-blocking effect, while celery is a good source of vitamin C, which also helps lower uric acid levels.

Lemon helps to bring the body into a more alkaline state, as it stimulates the formation of calcium carbonate that neutralizes acids such as uric acid.

Juice menu

Page 99: GO*ut* Getter

Superfood Booster

Wheatgrass or barley grass can help increase alkalinity and in turn increase uric acid solubility.

❀ Fertility and Conception

When I was trying to conceive my daughter Belle, I wanted to do everything in my power to create a fertile and healthy environment in which a tiny baby would flourish. Just like you would make sure the floors were vacuumed and there were clean sheets on the bed for a new houseguest, I took a similar approach to getting pregnant. My husband Leon and I had been traveling and working a lot, and felt a bit run-down, so I embarked on a three-day juice cleanse. Feeling re-energized, I went back to the books to learn about what dietary and lifestyle considerations I needed to make if I wanted an easy conception and pregnancy. When I met nutritional therapist and fertility/pregnancy specialist Henrietta Norton (see page 13), I loved her stats and advice about the importance of diet in conception, particularly the influential period in the three months leading up to conception. I shall pass the torch over to the expert to explain.

How can your diet support conception?

Nutrition is the fundamental issue for you and your baby. Studies have shown that couples who have made changes to their diet and lifestyle improved their chance of healthy conception by 80 percent, but research has also shown us that the benefits extend way beyond a healthy conception and pregnancy. Indeed, your nutritional status during the preconception period is now understood to sow the seeds of health for your growing baby in infancy, reducing, for instance, the risk of atopic conditions, such as asthma and eczema, as well as chronic health conditions like diabetes in adulthood.

For any of you who have been struggling with conceiving feel empowered that your diet can improve your chances of conception by 80 percent.

The three months prior to conception are thought to be the most influential. During this time, immature eggs, known as oocytes, mature enough to be released during ovulation, and sperm cells develop ready for ejaculation. You and your partner's nutrient intake greatly influences the quality and efficiency of this process and offers an opportunity to create a healthy pregnancy.

Over and above providing the healthy foundation stones, dietary changes and improving nutrient stores may also help to correct factors that may be affecting your ability to conceive, such as low sperm count or menstrual cycle hormonal imbalances.

Nourishing your nutritional status at preconception can also influence milk production during breastfeeding and reduce the potential of post-partum depression.

Let's get it sorted!
Support your liver

The hormonal balance needed for fertility depends on good liver function. Aside from its daily task of detoxifying substances such as caffeine and environmental toxins, it also chemically alters an excess of used hormones.

If this process doesn't happen effectively, hormonal imbalances can occur, affecting fertility and causing other health concerns such as endometriosis, acne, premenstrual syndrome (PMS), and polycystic ovary syndrome (PCOS). Many of Henrietta's clients have found that following a liver-cleansing program prior to conception has been highly beneficial.

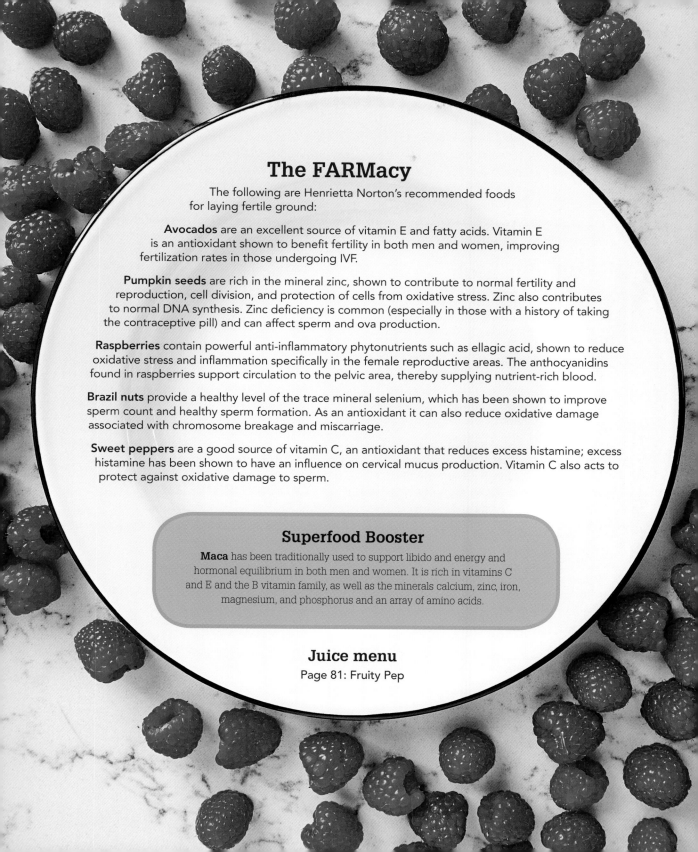

The FARMacy

The following are Henrietta Norton's recommended foods for laying fertile ground:

Avocados are an excellent source of vitamin E and fatty acids. Vitamin E is an antioxidant shown to benefit fertility in both men and women, improving fertilization rates in those undergoing IVF.

Pumpkin seeds are rich in the mineral zinc, shown to contribute to normal fertility and reproduction, cell division, and protection of cells from oxidative stress. Zinc also contributes to normal DNA synthesis. Zinc deficiency is common (especially in those with a history of taking the contraceptive pill) and can affect sperm and ova production.

Raspberries contain powerful anti-inflammatory phytonutrients such as ellagic acid, shown to reduce oxidative stress and inflammation specifically in the female reproductive areas. The anthocyanidins found in raspberries support circulation to the pelvic area, thereby supplying nutrient-rich blood.

Brazil nuts provide a healthy level of the trace mineral selenium, which has been shown to improve sperm count and healthy sperm formation. As an antioxidant it can also reduce oxidative damage associated with chromosome breakage and miscarriage.

Sweet peppers are a good source of vitamin C, an antioxidant that reduces excess histamine; excess histamine has been shown to have an influence on cervical mucus production. Vitamin C also acts to protect against oxidative damage to sperm.

Superfood Booster

Maca has been traditionally used to support libido and energy and hormonal equilibrium in both men and women. It is rich in vitamins C and E and the B vitamin family, as well as the minerals calcium, zinc, iron, magnesium, and phosphorus and an array of amino acids.

Juice menu

Page 81: Fruity Pep

High Cholesterol

High cholesterol is one of many risk factors that lead to hardening of the arteries and cardiovascular disease. Don't mess with it! We love talking cholesterol because it is one of the ailments you (in most circumstances) can have empowering control over by simply changing your diet. Which means? Yep, more magical fruits and veggies and less boxed crap. As there are so many efficient medications (know someone who is on statins?), many people opt to pop a pill rather than make dietary changes. I went to Dr. Nigma Talib (see page 13), to look at high cholesterol as a holistic problem and offer a holistic solution.

What is high cholesterol?

Cholesterol is a fatty substance in the body that fulfills several vital roles. High cholesterol occurs when "bad" cholesterol builds up in the blood. But "good" cholesterol does awesome things:

- It's a building block for various hormones, like estrogen in women and testosterone in men.
- It plays a major part in stabilizing the membranes or outer coating of the cells.
- It's a major component of the bile acid that helps digest our foods in the intestine.

Cholesterol heroes and losers

Cholesterol is transported in your blood by lipoproteins: HDL (high-density lipoprotein); LDL and VLDL (low- and very low-density lipoprotein). LDL and VLDL transport fats (primarily triglycerides and cholesterol) *from* the liver to the body cells (losers). Elevations of LDLs and VLDLs are associated with an increased risk of developing atherosclerosis, the primary cause of heart attack and stroke. HDL carries fats to the liver to be eliminated (hero!). Elevations of HDLs are associated with a low risk of heart attack.

Do you have it?

Cholesterol levels are important for good health, but if your blood cholesterol levels rise excessively, you are at increased risk of cardiovascular disease. Although genetics partly determine whether or not you are prone to high cholesterol, families also share lifestyle and eating habits. You are in control of your own destiny. Being vigilant about your diet and exercise plan can help you keep cholesterol levels in a happy place.

What's causing it?

Cholesterol levels are usually reflective of dietary and lifestyle factors, although it can also be due to genetic factors (thanks, Mom!).

Let's get it sorted!

Every one percent drop in LDL levels brings a two percent drop in the risk of heart attack. For every one percent increase in HDL, heart attack risk drops three to four percent. So use the equation below to your health advantage.

Cholesterol levels in your body are determined like this:

How much cholesterol your body makes (this is what differs because of genetic disposition) **+** How much cholesterol you take in from food **−** How much you eliminate **=** Your blood cholesterol levels

Eat less saturated fat

Reduce or eliminate the amounts of animal products, processed, fried, or refined foods in your diet.

Eat more fiber-rich plant foods

It's important to eat a variety of cholesterol-lowering vegetables, including celery, beet, eggplants, garlic, onions, sweet peppers, and root vegetables. In addition, dandelion root and Jerusalem artichoke contain the fiber inulin, which improves production of antioxidant enzymes, while decreasing total cholesterol and triglyceride levels and raising concentrations of beneficial HDL cholesterol.

Love your legumes

Diets rich in legumes, including peanuts, are effective in lowering cholesterol levels, and soy bean protein has been shown to be able to lower total cholesterol levels by 30 percent and LDL levels by as much as 35–40 percent.

Nibble on nuts and seeds

Nuts, particularly almonds and walnuts, and seeds are useful in lowering cholesterol and guarding against heart disease through their fiber, monounsaturated oil, and essential fatty acid content. Hazelnuts have exceptional concentrations of copper, a key component of superoxide dismutase, which disarms free radicals that would damage cholesterol and other lipids. Ground flax seed lowers two cholesterol-carrying molecules, apolipoprotein A-1 and B.

THE FARMacy

These are Dr. Nigma's recommendations for fruits and vegetables to help lower "bad" cholesterol (LDL):

Apples are rich in pectin that lowers LDL. People who eat two apples a day may lower their cholesterol by as much as 16 percent. The polyphenols in apples account for a lot of the cholesterol-reducing effect, due to their antioxidant activity.

Basil is a very good source of vitamin A through its concentration of carotenoids such as beta-carotene, which is converted into pro-vitamin A. The powerful antioxidant activity of basil also helps protect the blood vessel walls. Not only does that protect the epithelial cells (forming the lining of numerous body structures, blood vessels included) from free radical damage, it also helps prevent free radicals from oxidizing cholesterol in the bloodstream. (Only after it has been oxidized does cholesterol build up in blood vessel walls, initiating the development of atherosclerosis.) Basil is also a good source of magnesium, which prompts muscles and blood vessels to relax, improving blood flow and lessening the risk of irregular heart or blood vessel rhythms.

Coconut oil is a highly saturated fat but it's the oil least vulnerable to oxidative stress and free-radical formation. Because it contains medium-chain fatty acids, as opposed to long-chain ones in most fats/oils, it doesn't raise cholesterol levels and has been shown to lower LDL. Unprocessed virgin coconut oil contains a plant-based saturated fat called lauric acid that has been shown to boost HDL ("good" cholesterol).

Carrots: a cup of chopped raw carrot contains 3.6g of dietary fiber — more than 10 percent of the recommended daily allowance of 20–35g. Much of this is soluble fiber, which may reduce blood cholesterol. According to the University of Arizona College of Agriculture and Life Sciences, soluble fiber binds to bile acids, which contain cholesterol, and carries them through the gastrointestinal tract (see pages 15–16) to be excreted.

Juice menu

Page 91: Cholesterol Police

Superfood Booster

Turmeric contains curcumin, which may prevent the oxidation of cholesterol in the body (also see basil). It is also a good source of vitamin B6, needed to manage homocysteine, high levels of which are considered a significant risk factor for blood-vessel damage, atherosclerotic plaque build-up, and heart disease.

♥ High Blood Pressure

Do you like feeling as though you're pushed up against a wall? Well neither does the blood being pumped against your artery walls. If movie clichés were real, high blood pressure (or hypertension) would be a symptom suffered only by overweight, middle-aged men. *Au contraire!* According to the British Heart Foundation (in Britain) and the CDC (in America) nearly one in three men and women are being treated for high blood pressure. Dr. Nigma Talib (see page 13) explains what blood "pressure" really means, and how you can help combat it through your diet.

What is high blood pressure?

Your heart pumps blood throughout your body to supply it with oxygen and the energy it needs. As the blood moves, it pushes against the sides of the blood vessels and the strength at which it pushes is your blood pressure. If your blood pressure is too high, it puts extra strain on your arteries and your heart, and if hypertension is left untreated, it is a risk factor and increases your susceptibility to a heart attack and/or stroke.

Do you have it?

Below are the blood pressure measurements to watch out for:

Pre-hypertension (120–139/80–89)
Borderline   (120–160/90–94)
Mild   (140–160/95–104)
Moderate   (140–180/105–114)
Severe   (160+/115+)

Borderline to moderate high blood pressure is generally without symptoms, while severe hypertension may be associated with increased sleepiness, confusion, headache, nausea, and vomiting.

What's causing it?

The medical textbooks indicate that the cause of hypertension is unknown in 95 percent of patients. While genetics play a role in the cause, diet and lifestyle factors have been linked to high blood pressure. A diet that includes copious amounts of coffee, alcohol, sodium, sugar, and saturated fat and too little potassium, fiber, essential fatty acids, calcium, and magnesium from fresh fruits and vegetables increases your risk for hypertension. Additionally, if your lifestyle involves too little exercise but a lot of stress and if you smoke, your risk for hypertension increases.

Let's get it sorted!

See your doctor, and they will likely agree on the following steps:

Get moving

And that means doing at least 20 minutes exercise every day.

Make over your diet

Cut out the main culprits like sodium and saturated fats, and start adjusting your diet to include the foods from the magical plant kingdom that are mentioned opposite.

THE FARMacy

The following are Dr. Nigma's recommended fruits and vegetables for regulating blood pressure:

Celery calms the nerves because of its high calcium content and helps in controlling high blood pressure. It contains phytochemicals known as phthalides, which relax the muscle tissue in the artery walls, enabling increased blood flow and, in turn, lowering blood pressure.

Parsley contains flavonoids, especially luteolin, that have been shown to function as antioxidants in helping to prevent oxygen-based damage to cells, especially your blood vessels. In addition, parsley is rich in calcium and vitamins A and C, which can help to reduce blood pressure.

Beet juice contains about 0.2g of dietary nitrate. Nitrate is converted to a chemical called nitrite in the body, and then converted to nitric oxide in the blood. Nitric oxide is a gas that widens blood vessels and aids blood flow.

Broccoli contains an antioxidant called glucoraphanin that has demonstrated its ability to lower blood pressure and the risk of stroke and heart attack. In recent scientific experiments (see the Bibliography on page 143), rats that were fed a glucoraphanin-rich diet had a lowered inflammatory response and improved cardiovascular health, evidenced by decreased blood pressure and decreased inflammation in the heart, arteries, and kidneys.

Tomato juice contains several antioxidant substances, including lycopene, beta-carotene, vitamin C, and selenium. Tomatoes also have diuretic properties, which can help reduce blood pressure as well as enhance detoxification of the liver and kidneys.

Juice menu

Page 100: Hypertension Hero

Superfood Booster

Spinach really is a superfood, so Popeye was ahead of the game! I can't emphasize enough the need for spinach in our diet, given that our modern diet is in general deficient in folic acid, fiber, and essential vitamins and minerals. It is as a result of not consuming enough dark green leaf vegetables, and spinach in particular, that we are prone to developing cardiovascular disease due to the risk factor of homocysteine (see page 41), which increases over time if we continue to lack these nutrients.

Low Sex Drive

There are few things more depressing or frustrating than feeling low on mojo; it's an instant downer to feel lack of stamina and sexual desire, especially if you consider yourself a healthy person. Low libido or loss of interest in sexual activity is usually rationalized into self-doubts such as "I'm not attracted by my partner anymore" or "I'm too busy with life/work/kids." Surprisingly, researchers have found that 90 percent of reported sexual dysfunction, in both men and women, is not due to emotional blocks, as many conclude, but an actual medical issue more often than not related to diet!

What's causing it?

The truth is that low sex drive can have many causes, among the most common being cardiovascular disease, high LDL ("bad" cholesterol) and clogged arteries, high blood pressure, obesity, diabetes, or all of the above combined into something called metabolic syndrome. Low sex drive/performance can also be caused by depression, though it should cease once depression clears. Hormonal imbalances can also affect sexual desire, as can the use of prescription medication, a very common yet often ignored cause — always check the side-effects on medication labels.

Let's get it sorted!

Brush up your cv system

The key to improving sex drive and performance is a healthy cardiovascular system. Actually, doctors agree that one of the earliest signs of cardiovascular disease in men is decreased sexual performance. If you think about it, this is pretty major because it means that sexual dysfunction offers an insight into what's going on inside the small blood vessels in the whole body (i.e. clogged, inflamed, hardened) even before hard evidence is revealed through lab work or X-rays. Our sexual organs and tissues are lined with small blood vessels or capillaries through which blood and nutrients flow so that things can work optimally "down there."

Detox and nourish

We know that diets high in processed foods, animal products, saturated or trans fats, and refined carbohydrates can deteriorate and clog our arteries, but the first line of severe damage happens at the level of these small capillaries (especially the ones "down there"). So first and foremost, to improve your sex drive and performance, it's crucial that you ditch eating junk and initiate a detox program to clean your gut so that you can absorb all the nutrients you need to perform like a rockstar.

THE FARMacy

These are dietitian Romina Pulichino's (see page 11) recommended fruits and vegetables to help you regain mojo:

Spinach, lentils, watermelon, and pomegranate are great sources of arginine. Nitric oxide (NO) is a molecule that relaxes blood vessels and increases blood flow, promoting engorgement of sexual organ tissues. To produce NO, you need the amino acid arginine, and this is *so* important in keeping good amounts of nitric oxide pumping that the mechanism of Viagra™ is designed around prolonging its effects in the body. These veg and fruit sources of arginine have an advantage over animal sources in that they contain antioxidants such as vitamins C and E and zinc, among many others, which help prevent toxins from destroying the nitric oxide and keep vessel walls toned, smooth, and damage free.

Celery is another readily available food that can help you in the bedroom. Used since Roman times as an aphrodisiac, celery contains androstenone and androstenol, pheromones that boost your sexual arousal and send the brain sexy signals that stimulate desire from you to others and others to you. Bingo! Celery also contains calcium and magnesium, essential minerals for relaxation and contraction of muscles (you'll need that, too).

Juice menu

Page 80: Snake Charmer

Superfood Booster

Maca is one of the oldest superfoods known to increase energy and sexual stamina, and works on the body's sexual glands to optimize hormonal production. Maca contains many other natural chemicals such as free fatty acids, amino acids, and vitamins essential for the health of the reproductive organs.

Fading Fitness Performance

A lot of our regular juicers are, unsurprisingly, frequent exercisers. Immediate side-effects of exercise include improvements in mood, heart health, sexual performance, and clearer skin. We say "heck yeah" to all of these, and think a healthy diet and exercise regime are the ultimate keys to the wellness kingdom. We often get asked, "Which juice should I drink before a workout?" or "What's the best juice to follow a workout?" There are many considerations that go into answering these questions responsibly. I thought it would be helpful to give you a breakdown of what your body needs before and after your workout, so that your inner physician can prescribe you the correct juice. Eve Kalinik (see page 12) gives us the full download here.

How can your diet support your fitness performance?

It's likely that you've clocked professional athletes following a strict nutrition plan before, during, and after a game, which ensures that they have provided their bodies with the correct fuel to optimize their fitness performance when it's game time. Just like the pros, your own fitness performance can be affected by many factors ranging from the level of your pre-training, your recovery techniques, and of course the quality (good or bad) of your nutrition. If you don't eat the right foods to support your fitness, you can feel weak and tired, and could be more prone to injury and illness. It's therefore important to give your body all the necessary tools to be able to gain the best results and enable the most efficient recovery.

Let's get it sorted!

Fuel up on slow-release energy

Carbohydrate, which is broken down into glucose, is the body's main fuel for sustaining endurance and performance, particularly in any long-distance events. Glycogen is the storage form of glucose that has been broken down and mostly stored in the liver (a small amount can be stored in muscle tissue, too). When these levels are too low, your exercise potential can be adversely affected. The best sources of carbohydrate are those that offer a slow release of energy, such as vegetables and wholegrains like quinoa, spelt, and brown rice (not the refined white stuff that we typically associate with this group).

Train and recoup with premium protein

Protein is necessary for training and recovery, and requirements depend on the intensity and the duration of the exercise. A good guide to your daily target is around 1g of protein for every 2¼lb of body weight. Protein is needed to help restore and repair muscle tissue during training and it's important to include plenty of good-quality sources in the diet, such as organic free-range eggs, legumes, nuts and seeds, organic free-range chicken, wild-caught fish, and organic, grass-fed meats (in moderation!).

Aid recovery with healthy oils

Fats from healthy oils found in the omega-3 family, such as oily fish, chia seeds, and flax seeds (linseeds) can be beneficial in helping to support recovery, aiding in anti-inflammatory processes and nourishing cell membranes for increased flexibility and cell performance.

Drink smart

Hydration is also key, since fluid loss reduces performance and endurance. Replacement of essential nutrients, such as sodium, potassium, calcium, and magnesium, is crucial.

Restore and repair with antioxidants

Antioxidants can be beneficial for post-exercise recovery to help mop up the free radicals generated during activity and to help repair tissues. Find these in foods rich in vitamins C, A, and E and zinc, such as Swiss chard, kiwi fruit, blueberries, carrots, romaine lettuce, sweet peppers, sweet potatoes, tomatoes, nuts, and seeds.

Notch up your nutrients

Other nutrients that are essential for energy-yielding metabolism include the full spectrum of B vitamins, found in lentils, wholegrains, almonds, asparagus, spinach, and avocados. Magnesium and calcium are necessary minerals for muscle and nerve functioning; look to leafy greens, sesame seeds, figs, broccoli, bok choy, and okra. Iron, vital for the formation of hemoglobin and efficient transport of oxygen around the body and into muscle cells, can be found in nuts and seeds, legumes, and organic grass-fed meats.

THE FARMacy

These are Eve's recommended fruits and vegetables for maximizing your workouts:

Beet is a good source of iron, which helps to support stamina and endurance for sustained performance. Beet also contain significant levels of folic acid, part of the B group of vitamins, important for metabolic processes. Its other winning nutrient is nitrate, which converts into nitrite and then nitric oxide in the body. This helps to widen blood vessels and increase blood flow, as well as reducing the oxygen needed by the muscles so that they can work more efficiently.

Superfood Booster

Chlorophyll is the compound that makes green veggies green (see pages 20–21). Its chemical structure is similar to hemoglobin, which helps transport oxygen around the body and into muscle cells. Add liquid chlorophyll to juices or load up on leafy greens

Leafy greens such as kale, chard, romaine lettuce, and spinach are other sources of iron, but they also contain vitamins A and C, which have antioxidant properties, helping to mop up free radicals generated during exercise. Spinach also contains zinc, which helps to reduce lactic acid levels and is readily lost in sweat.

Cucumber is hydrating with its high water content and contains electrolytes lost during exercise. Coconut water is another source of electrolyte replacement, helping to rebalance post-activity. It also contains readily available natural sugars for instant refuel.

Ginger can provide anti-inflammatory properties and promote circulation to help reduce muscle soreness post-exercise.

Chia seeds are an excellent source of omega-3, helping to reduce inflammation, and they provide protein for muscle recovery and repair.

Himalayan salt packs in over 80 minerals and elements, in particular sodium chloride, lost during exercise. Because of its mineral content, this pink salt can help to rebalance electrolytes, increase hydration, and prevent muscle cramping.

Juice menu

Page 64: Green Recovery
Page 75: Fitness Fuel

Arthritis

Arthritis is something that runs in my family, and I've watched how family members on my maternal side have to deal with its debilitating effects. My super mama Patti is an inspiration. She refuses to let arthritis slow her down and has been quite successful at "getting ahead" of it with a mix of exercise and some diet tweaks. On her 60th birthday, she signed up for her first marathon, and now, nearly 70, continues to run five miles every day and play on her local tennis team with women 30 years her junior. Go Patti, go Patti!

What is arthritis?

Osteoarthritis (OA) is a degenerative disease that results in swelling, stiffness, pain, and sometimes deformity in the (most commonly) weight-bearing joints, such as the hands, feet, knees, and hips. In a healthy joint, the bone itself will be coated with cartilage (a tough, rubbery connective tissue) that absorbs shock, reduces friction, and allows the bones to glide against each other during movement. In a joint with osteoarthritis, there is a breakdown of the cartilage, resulting in a chronic inflammatory response and an increase in free radicals that directly destroy the cartilage and the membrane around it. In order to stabilize the joint, the bone can grow to compensate for the empty space, and flexibility and fluidity of movement can be compromised. As the cartilage starts to wear away, the bones grind together (without any protection from the shock-absorbing cartilage), creating pain and further restricting movement.

What's causing it?

Attributable causes of OA include wear and tear, obesity, diabetes, food sensitivities or allergies, trauma to the joint itself, osteoporosis (loss of bony tissue), genetic factors, or neuromuscular disorders. Hormonal and metabolic conditions may also have an impact. The prevailing view in the medical community attributes the condition to lifelong wear and tear on the joints. A recent study by the Stanford University School of Medicine offered hopeful findings that by targeting the inflammatory processes that occur in the early stages of osteoarthritis (before symptoms appear), the condition may one day be preventable.

Let's get it sorted!

Choose the foods that soothe

Helping to reduce and manage inflammatory responses is essential in this condition, so a diet that features plenty of anti-inflammatory foods, such as those rich in omega-3 including oily fish, chia seeds, and flax seeds (linseeds), can be beneficial. Increasing antioxidant foods in the diet can also help alleviate symptoms. Foods high in antioxidants include vitamin C- and E-rich foods, such as broccoli, kale, spinach, sweet peppers, cabbage, cauliflower, nuts, seeds, and avocados.

Lose the foods that offend

Reducing inflammatory foods in the diet is equally important, as well as taking account of any food sensitivities or allergies that may be exacerbating the condition. Often it can be the regular offenders (wheat, gluten, dairy, or soy) but there is some evidence that foods high in amines can increase symptoms. These are often found in wine, beer, aged, overcooked, and processed meats, aged or blue cheese, soy sauce, dried fruits, and chocolate, and they should be avoided, especially if you notice a link.

Take a daily dose of sunshine

Vitamin D deficiency has additionally been associated with OA, so a prescription of ten minutes' sunshine per day or including vitamin

D-fortified plant milks in your diet are good ways of making sure you keep these levels well maintained.

The FARMacy

These are Eve Kalinik's (see page 12) recommended foods for helping to prevent and manage arthritis:

Kale, broccoli, and spinach are all excellent sources of vitamin C, which has an anabolic building affect on cartilage and is required to help regenerate bone cells. Its antioxidant properties are also useful in reducing oxidative inflammatory reactions and to help mop up free radicals. These veggies also contain some level of vitamin E, another antioxidant that also helps to stabilize membranes and plays a role in inhibiting the initial damaging process.

Celery is another great source of vitamin C and also a natural diuretic, helping to stimulate urination and the elimination of toxins.

Pineapple contains bromelain, which has been shown to have some anti-inflammatory and analgesic properties that can help reduce pain and inflammation.

Juice menu

Page 66: Tropical Greens

Superfood Booster

Turmeric helps reduce inflammation and also supports antioxidant activity and detoxification.

⏰ Insomnia

How many sheep have you counted in your life? You may not be alone, as there is evidence that many of us have taken medication to fall asleep. This can be useful for resetting a sleep pattern, particularly for an acute problem like dealing with grief, but for a long-term solution, we want to help you sort out the root of the problem. With some relaxation tips, and a few recommended dietary tweaks from Eve Kalinik (see page 12), we hope you're already falling asleep reading this page.

What is insomnia?

Insomnia, or sleeplessness, is the inability to fall or stay asleep and is experienced either for a short period or for many people on a chronic basis. Insomnia can be categorized into two broader types: sleep onset insomnia, referring to difficulty falling asleep, or sleep maintenance insomnia, which means frequent or early waking. The long-term effects of insomnia can lead to depression, diabetes, cardiovascular disease, poor memory, and impaired immune system function.

Do you have it?

The most common symptoms include difficulty initiating sleep and waking throughout the night or waking early with an inability to fall back to sleep. Sufferers will also find that they are excessively tired, and basic functioning and everyday skills may be affected.

What's causing it?

Possible causes of sleep onset insomnia can include increased levels of anxiety, pain, stimulants, or even your bedroom environment — being too hot or having too much light are common culprits. Sleep maintenance insomnia can be attributed to factors such as hypoglycemia (glucose deficiency), sleep apnea (interrupted breathing), depression, or even to high circulating levels of the stress hormone cortisol.

Let's get it sorted!

Exercise

Incorporating exercise early into your day gives you an outlet for the release of tension that might otherwise be burning you up as soon as you try to relax. Exercise also releases endorphins that may help mellow out your nerves and anxiety.

Avoid stimulants

Coffee, caffeinated teas, and sugar can all interfere with your sleep cycle, making it difficult for you to fall asleep. Caffeine can affect your sleep for up to 24 hours, so try to lose it completely, or limit it to the morning. Replace your afternoon tea or coffee with a fresh juice or herbal tea and nutm*lk (see pages 102–107) for a more sustainable energy boost.

Lose the booze and big dinners

Alcohol and a big meal may help you fall asleep initially but will interrupt your sleep cycle, causing you to wake in the night.

Introduce sleep-friendly foods

A diet rich in tryptophan can increase levels of serotonin, the precursor to melatonin. Melatonin is a hormone that helps to regulate circadian (daily) rhythms and govern sleep–wake cycles. Food sources include eggs, sesame seeds, organic free-range chicken, cashew nuts, almonds, bananas, and chickpeas. Low glucose levels can also impair sleep, so ensuring that your final meal of the day is a good combination of protein and carbohydrates will help to maintain more consistent blood glucose levels during the night.

Don't overindulge

Avoid stimulants such as caffeine and refined sugar after mid-afternoon, swapping out that coffee with a juice, and don't eat heavy meals late in the evening. Removing all equipment such as Wi-Fi and laptops at night reduces excess exposure to electromagnetic fields and can also promote sleep. Instead, make your bedroom a sanctuary by adding a few drops of lavender oil to your pillow, lulling you into a relaxed and restful night ahead.

The FARMacy

In addition to the sleep-friendly foods listed opposite, the following foods aid sleep:

Spinach, romaine lettuce, kale, and broccoli are excellent sources of folic acid, magnesium, and vitamins B6 and C, which are all key co-factors in neurotransmitter functioning. Spinach and parsley also contain glutamine, which is an important precursor in these pathways.

Superfood Booster

Sour cherry juice is a source of melatonin, the hormone that regulates our sleep patterns. Just a dash will be enough!

Juice menu

Page 74: Mellow Garden

 Struggling Skin Health

The beauty business is a multibillion-dollar industry. Whether you're combatting something as chronic as psoriasis or on a lifelong search for the perfect cream to erase the signs of aging, your skin will benefit if you start feeding it wisely. With a combination of proper nutrition, hydration, and clean beauty, everyone will be asking how you maintain your gorgeous glow!

What does skin health mean?

Skin is the largest and one of the most important body organs. It battles daily with exposure to toxins from pollution, sun damage, and chemicals, which can all contribute to poor skin health and deterioration in skin quality — in other words, premature wrinkles. Your skin is the first line of defence against the environment, like a natural armor, and it is therefore important to make sure it's supple and strong. The skin consists of two layers — the epidermis and dermis — and below that a layer of subcutaneous fat. The epidermis is replaced approximately every 40 days, so with the right ingredients (literally), you can improve the quality of your skin in just over a month.

Do you have poor skin health?

Eczema or psoriasis, through to acne, wrinkles, and earlier-than-expected sagging are signs that your skin may need a bit of TLC from the inside out. Symptoms are painful, dry, and flaky skin, an excess of oil production leading to pimples and breakouts, or thinning of the skin.

What's causing it?

Our very own glow-getter Eve Kalinik (see page 12), says that often the symptoms of poor skin health can indicate a lack of nutrients or a struggling digestive system, such as absorption problems or an imbalance of beneficial "good" bacteria in the digestive system. More directly, it can also be linked to a diet that is high in acidic-forming inflammatory foods such as meat, dairy, alcohol, and caffeine, which alter the body's natural slightly alkaline environment and allow those lesser-friendly bacteria to thrive (see page 17). Skin membranes also need to be hydrated to remain strong and supple. Not drinking enough water can leave the skin thirsty. If the detoxification pathways in the body are overloaded, this can also result in unpleasant skin symptoms.

Let's get it sorted!

Drink that juice

For clear, healthy skin, drinking fresh juices can act as a simple and effective way to hydrate, at the same time as stimulating and supporting the detoxification process.

Nourish your skin with nutrients

You can look to achieve a radiant complexion by taking in nutrients that promote good skin health. Yes, you can eat (or drink!) your way to a more glowing visage. This includes packing in lots of vitamin C-rich foods such as sweet peppers, chiles, broccoli, kale, and spinach, as well as vitamin A-rich foods including sweet potatoes, carrots, butternut squash, dandelion greens, and Swiss chard. Zinc is another key player, as it helps to regulate sebum production and assist in the structure of skin cell membranes, and you can find this in pumpkin seeds, cashew nuts, and raw cacao. And healthy oils such as those found in omega-3s and -6s are essential in helping to nourish the skin cell membranes as well as supporting anti-inflammatory processes in the body. These are present in oily fish, chia seeds and flax seeds (linseeds).

Out with the old

Incorporate exfoliation in your skincare regime. Removing dead skin cells allows for easier detoxification, and reveals a fresher, newer batch of cells ready to glow. Use a body brush at least three times a week on dry skin before your shower. If you wash your face with a cloth, you probably only need to exfoliate your face once a week, but if you're washing just with cleanser and water, exfoliating two or three times a week will remove makeup debris, allow for proper detoxification, and eliminate dead skin cells from the surface.

The FARMacy

Broccoli and spinach are great sources of folic acid and vitamin C, which are both essential for cell regeneration and repair. Vitamin C also supports the process of collagen formation and works to reduce oxidative damage. Furthermore, these greens contain the antioxidant beta-carotene, which can assist detoxification processes and minimize toxin build-up in the body. They are also rich in vitamin A, important for healthy cell replication and differentiation.

Fennel is also an excellent source of vitamin C, but probably the most unique component of this root veg is the phytonutrient anethole. This compound has been shown to reduce inflammation and contains natural anti-microbial properties, which help balance bacteria in the gastrointestinal tract and in turn promote detoxification.

Apples are packed with phytonutrients, which means that they have antioxidant properties that help to scavenge free radicals. They also contain the flavonoid quercetin, which can inhibit enzymes that convert complex carbohydrates into simple sugars, so in this sense they help to regulate blood sugar levels. This is important in skin health, as spikes in blood sugar can damage collagen.

Cilantro is a remarkable heavy metal detoxifier (or chelator), helping to bind and remove heavy metals from the body and so act as a detoxing support. It also has antibacterial and antifungal properties, which help to balance gut microflora. After all, healthy digestion = a happy complexion.

Cucumber, often underrated as a superfood, is one of the most hydrating of veggies. It contains almost 95 percent water and important electrolytes. It also provides B vitamins and a wealth of minerals, as well as potent antioxidant properties.

Juice menu

Page 69: Green Glow-getter

Superfood Booster

Aloe vera juice helps soothe and promote the growth of beneficial bacteria in the digestive system, while reducing general acidity in the body. It is also an adaptogen, which means that it boosts the body's natural ability to cope with external changes and outside stresses.

For the Love of Juice

Do you ever wish you could erase the effects of how you have treated your body in the past? The good news is you may be able to (well, sort of).

If you've had too many big nights to count or years gone by with more ready meals than homemade meals, there is much scientific evidence to suggest that what you put into your body today gives you opportunity to discard damaged cells from the past and to start anew.

Most people think of their body, and the cells that it is composed of, as a relatively permanent structure. On the contrary — most cells are regularly discarded and new ones are produced to replace them. Each tissue in your body (heart, stomach, skin) takes a different period of time to fully regenerate, but on average, every seven years you have a new set of cells and your own proverbial clean slate.

Knowing what you know now, you can see how essential it is to use the purest, most amazing raw materials as building blocks for your new cells. Your body can actually feel better and younger and look better as you age. Motivated?

Here's where the juice comes in

We now know that eating raw vegetables and fruits increases energy, prevents chronic illnesses, promotes an alkaline pH, and helps rebuild your cells so that they are strong and healthy. We rarely eat enough fresh veggies and fruits, and this is where the juice comes in! Would you be able to eat eight whole kale leaves, one large cucumber, a bunch of parsley, a head of lettuce, two apples, a lemon, a large handful of spinach, and a piece of ginger in one sitting? Probably not, but you can drink it all in a single glass of juice. The bottom line is that the more fresh vegetables and fruits you consume, the lower your risk of becoming ill or dying prematurely. Oh, and you'll look and feel better too!

Intravenous nutrition

Juicing is a great way to expedite the delivery of superfoods to your bloodstream. Juicing extracts the vitamins, minerals, antioxidants, chlorophyll, enzymes, and phytochemicals from fruits and vegetables in a liquid form. By removing the soluble fiber, your body can absorb these nutrients almost instantly and by removing the fiber, you're outsourcing the job of digestion to your juicer and giving your overworked digestive system a break, while offering it an intravenous drip of nutrition straight to your cells. When you drink a fresh juice, your body is able to assimilate the nutrients within 15 minutes, compared to a solid meal that may take over 2 hours to get to your cells. This gives your body an abundance of clean, green, and nutrient-dense building blocks to a healthier version of you.

When to juice and when to cleanse?

A juice a day keeps the doctor away!

I recommend having at least one 1 pint (2 cup) glass of green juice every single day for the rest of your long, healthy life (see pages 62–77). Drink a green juice first thing in the morning, pre-coffee and food, and see how your body sings. I am pretty confident that you will no longer need coffee to wake up and your cells will crave that emerald green liquid instead. Depending on how your body feels and how many vegetables you're able to consume in your everyday life, you may find you need a second juice in the afternoon. If you've already had a green juice, by all means have another or venture into one of the root juices or fruit juices (see pages 78–101) to get the full spectrum of nutrients.

Cleansing

In an ideal world, everyone should cleanse once a month, but we know that's not always possible. Try scheduling in a cleanse at the change of each season, and then augment when you are feeling run-down, have a cold, need a hard stop from a period of overindulgence, or just need a reboot. We have a whole section in this book on creating your own cleanse (see page 108–137), or you can always order one from www.plenishcleanse.com or your local organic juice cleanse company and have it delivered to your door if you are short on time. The Pressed Juice Directory (www.pressedjuicedirectory.com), started by my friend Max Gerson in New York, is a great way of finding an organic, cold-pressed juice in any city around the world.

Choosing a juicer

Among juicing enthusiasts, the discussion on which juicer is best can get as heated as the fieriest political discussions. Depending on your vigor, budget, and tolerance for the time it takes to make a juice, there are a few considerations. For example, a ten percent difference in the yield (the amount of juice you get from your produce) is likely to be of less importance than the quality of the juice or how user-friendly the juicing and cleaning processes (i.e. how many parts to wash) are, so make sure those aspects are up there in your selection criteria. There is no point in investing in a super-expensive piece of kit if you never use it because it's a chore to clean.

There are three main types of juicer:

1. Cold presses

The mac daddy or Rolls-Royce of juicers is a cold press, called the Norwalk Juicer. It's what we use in our commercial operation at PLENISH and uses two stainless steel plates powered by hydraulic pressure to squeeze the living daylights out of a piece of fruit or veg. Because the press is so powerful, you end up with a very nutrient-dense juice, and as there is no heat, many of the enzymes are preserved. The reality is, I don't know anyone who has a Norwalk at home, as it's just too expensive (with a $2,500 price tag). When we developed the recipes in this book, we used a masticating and centrifugal juicer to test them and they were all delicious. So unless you hit the jackpot, I would recommend purchasing one of those instead.

2. Centrifugal juicers

Traditionally, this is the most common type of juicer that you've no doubt seen at your local department store, juice bar, or supermarket. They have spinning metal blades that spin against a mesh basket filter, separating the juice from the produce via centrifugal force. These juicers have a wide range of price points, but can be quite affordable and are quick at extracting the juice, hence why you find them in commercial juice bar settings. The slight downside with centrifugal juicers is that the blades generate heat and the spinning mechanism also introduces oxygen, which destroys some of the enzymes and more fragile nutrients. The heat also oxidizes those nutrients, rendering less nutritious juice than a cold press or slow (masticating) juicer.

3. Masticating juicers

Masticating juicers usually have a higher price point, but do produce a higher-quality juice. Masticating (or chewing) juicers extract juice by first crushing and then pressing fruit and vegetables for the highest juice yield. Because it's a slower process, the motor doesn't generate as much heat or oxygen in the process, so more of the nutrients are retained intact.

There is a new development on the masticating juicer, which is the vertical slow juicer. These masticating juicers are at the high end of the price scale, but are one of my top picks for juicing at home. They are usually dishwasher safe, which is a mega bonus in the cleaning criterion.

Tips on buying produce

Now you've found your juicer, you'll need produce for juicing. Here are a few handy shopping tips I've picked up along the way:

- Ripe produce has the highest level of antioxidants and the phytonutrients are at their peak.
- Look for ripe or nearly ripe fruits that are still firm. Apples, pears, and tomatoes that have gone soft turn into mush in the juicer and don't give a good yield, nor a nice-tasting juice.
- When shopping for greens, make sure there are no black leaves or slimy bits, or that they have gone dry and pale. These are past their peak and you want FRESH! Pale green spinach leaves have a lower level of vitamin C than vibrant ones.
- Buy organic. The organic food industry is strictly regulated by limiting the use of pesticides to fight off potential pests. These chemicals can be damaging to human health and wildlife, and are found in worrying amounts in non-organic produce. Organic food is also free of genetically modified (GM) factors.
- Organic vegetables and fruits come at a higher price, so prioritizing which you buy can help you mix and match and keep costs down. Ask the growers at your local farmers' market if they use pesticides. Many of them won't. This can be a great cost-effective, local option.

The Dirty Dozen and Clean Fifteen

Not all non-organic fruits and vegetables have a high pesticide level. Some produce has a natural protective layer that provides a defense against sprayed pesticides. If a fruit or veg has a thin skin (like a berry or apple) where you eat its "outer layer," you will also be ingesting the chemicals that were sprayed to keep pests away. When eating something like an avocado or banana, its outer layer gets discarded, so the inside has been protected to an extent.

The Dirty Dozen

Apples | Blueberries | Celery | Cherries | Cucumbers | Grapes | Lettuce | Nectarines | Peaches | Peppers | Spinach, kale, and collard greens | Strawberries

The Clean Fifteen

Asparagus | Avocados | Cabbage | Cantaloupe melon | Corn | Eggplant | Grapefruit | Kiwi fruit | Mangos | Onions | Papaya | Peas | Pineapple | Sweet potatoes | Watermelon

Ingredient superstars

Plant-based foods rock. I love to eat them, I love to juice them, and they are all special and wonderful. You will notice a few recurring ingredients (or superstars) that pop up in many of our recipes. This is not to say that all vegetables and fruits are not amazing healthy options, but this crew delivers a nutrient-packed punch to any juice and I recommend always having these guys handy.

Greens

Leafy greens provide more nutrients than any other natural food.

Kale — Although kale has been around since the Dark Ages, it's only recently had its moment in the spotlight because of its superfood status. Calorie for calorie, it has more iron than red meat and more calcium than milk. This makes it important for cell growth, transporting oxygen around the body, and strong bones. It's also chock-full of antioxidants and vitamin K, helping to protect against a wide variety of cancers. A great detox food, providing fiber and sulfur to support your liver.

Spinach — Popeye was ahead of his time. Little did he know that in addition to making his muscles strong, spinach may have helped protect him against cancer, macular degeneration, and inflammation thanks to the high levels of chlorophyll (see pages 20–21) and carotenoids. You would be hard pressed to find a plant-based food richer in vitamin K for healthy bones than spinach, and, like kale, it's rich in iron, as well as vitamin C (which helps with the iron absorption) to improve the function of red blood cells in transporting oxygen around the body.

Cucumber — Cukes are, in fact, from the same botanical family as melons. Because of their high water content (over 95 percent), they provide a great base for any juice. They are also very low in sugar and contribute a valuable array of vitamins and minerals. The potassium in cucumbers makes them effective in post-workout recovery support for hydration and electrolyte balance, and just half a cucumber will deliver nearly ten percent of your daily requirement of vitamin K. It also helps promote clear skin. Cucumber juice has a refreshing, slightly sweet taste, and mixes well with any green vegetable or fruit. As a regular juicer, I recommend always having fresh cucumbers on hand. Run cucumbers through the juicer last. Their high water content will "wash" through the bits of leafy greens you've already juiced. If you're not buying organic, make sure you peel them before you juice them.

Roots

Beet — Beet works hard for its superfood title. The rich purple color comes from its unique source of phytonutrient known as betacyanin, which offers antioxidant, anti-inflammatory, and detoxification support. Beet also provide a rich source of potassium, manganese, iron, vitamins A, B6, and C, and particularly folic acid. It has been linked with increased levels of stamina, improved blood flow, and lowering of blood pressure. After an article in *The New York Times* reported that cyclists who drank 2 cups of beet juice before a race were significantly faster and more powerful than when they rode "unjuiced," due to increased oxygen flow to muscles, there has been a focus on the use of beet juice in improving sports performance. It was those who drank beet juice regularly (rather than those consuming pre-race only) that saw the best results, so be(et) consistent. Drink beet juice like a glass of fine wine. Never chug, particularly if you are new to it, as it's a potent detoxifier and can make you ill if you consume it too quickly. It also stains, so take off your crisp, white shirt.

Carrots — Orange and crunchy, carrots are full of beta-carotene (a phytochemical that the body turns into vitamin A), whose antioxidant properties can help with functions such as vision, reproduction, healthy cell membranes, and growth, along with a host of other powerful antioxidants. Carrots have a very high water content (up to 85 percent) and are naturally sweet, so can help sweeten a juice without the need to add sugar. Carrot and a splash of lime provide a great counterbalance if you've gone overboard with beet in your recipe and need to mellow the flavor.

Sweet potatoes — The white potato's healthy counterpart is a nutrient-dense favorite of ours. Fear not carbo-phobes, with ample essential vitamins and minerals like vitamin C and the B complex, it can help protect against free radical damage in the body, while potassium (more than in bananas), magnesium, and copper promote healthy blood pressure and taut skin and muscles. Sweet potatoes make a great base for a filling juice. When juicing sweet potato, a white, starchy sediment gathers at the bottom; just pour off the juice and discard the sediment.

Fruits

Hands down, fruit juices taste delicious, but consume them sparingly in proportion to vegetable-based juices to keep sugar consumption under control. Here are a few of our favorites that perform low to medium on the GI chart (see page 25), to make sure your juice doesn't leave you with a spike in blood sugar, while offering some amazing health-promoting benefits and recipe versatility.

Apples — Raw apple juice is a great source of the antioxidant vitamin C, which promotes immunity and protects cells from damage caused by free radicals. Apple skin is rich in quercetin, a natural antioxidant that protects the colon. One of my favorite go-to natural sweeteners, apples mix well with both greens and roots.

Pears — An excellent source of vitamins B2, C, and E, copper, potassium, and the water-soluble fiber pectin, pears promote healthy cholesterol levels and tone the intestines for healthy digestion and elimination. Pears work really well to balance out strong green flavors like kale and broccoli if you are new to greens and need a bit more sweet camouflage.

Pineapple — Pineapples buck the norm in their GI rating. Most fruit juices rank higher on the GI chart compared to their whole food counterparts, but pineapple juice averages around 43 versus the whole food at 66. As a great source of the enzyme bromelain, pineapple juice aids digestion and promotes healthy bones and joints. They are also chock-full of vitamins and minerals like vitamins A–C as well as manganese, copper, and folate. Fresh-pressed juice tastes like a tropical treat, and is a great addition to a vegetable-based juice if you are craving a sweet snack, although I usually eat half of mine before it makes it into the juicer!

Juice Recipes

Tips for making juice

Keep it clean

Thoroughly wash all leafy veg, salad greens, and herbs and any fruits and veg that are juiced with their skins on.

Pack heavy

1 cup = tightly packed. Chop up that pineapple or broccoli (stems and all) and squish down that spinach or parsley to pack it densely. I used a standard measuring cup, but you can use a bowl or mug of the same capacity (½ pint). No excuses, this should be easy peasy.

Prep talk

Most fruits and veg can be juiced whole; some need a little prep. Top beets, strawberries, radishes, carrots; peel garlic, onions, pineapple, kiwis, papaya, avocados, and melons; remove peel and pith from citrus fruits, stalks, seeds, and pits from fruits, and seeds from peppers and chiles. Horseradish, ginger, and lemon grass are fine just the way they are.

Slow and steady wins the race

Cut up produce based on the size of the "mouth" of your juicer. Try to shove it all in, the juicer will jam. Promise.

Dry, then wet

Juice leafy greens and herbs first, followed by juicy fruits or water-based veg to wash through the bits.

When in doubt, add veg

Recipes make 2 cups, based on medium-size veg or fruits. Because of natural size variations, you may make a bit more or less. To bulk up a juice, add cucumber, zucchini, or lettuce. These are low in naturally-occurring sugar but high in vitamin-infused water content.

Don't have separation anxiety

Juices separate on standing. A gentle shake or stir will see you right.

Put a lid on it and chill out

Juices are best consumed within 24 hours. Store in an airtight container and refrigerate until use.

Sweet and Easy Greens

Fruits included to ease you in

Green Recovery

This is an extremely satisfying juice for any time of day, but especially after a workout. It's a beautiful deep green color too. If you are making this juice in advance, make sure to shake it vigorously, as the chia seeds will clump at the bottom. The coconut water and chia are chock-full of protein and electrolytes — vital minerals such as sodium, potassium, and magnesium that can be lost through sweating. The chlorophyll-rich greens also help eliminate any lactic acid build-up.

3 cups chard | 3 cups romaine lettuce | 2 cups broccoli pieces (florets and stems) |
1 cup coconut water | 1 tbsp chia seeds | pinch of Himalayan salt

Beachside Popeye

Popeye knew a thing or two about what to eat for healthy energy, and toted spinach as his vitamin A and iron booster. We envision this mild, easy green as what Popeye drinks on holiday!

1 cup spinach | 3–4 broccoli florets and stems | 2 celery sticks |
¼ cup cilantro | ¼ cup coconut water | 1 cucumber

Rad Green Juice

True to its name, this juice is totally rad. Radishes stimulate bile production, which aids in detoxification, and can be used as a low-sugar alternative to cranberries in treating discomfort from urinary tract infections. Mixed with the protein from the sprouts, this alkalizing, slightly sweet juice has a nice refreshing kick.

½ cup red radishes (trimmed) | ½ cup alfalfa or sunflower sprouts | 1 red apple (stalk removed) |
1 cup chard | 1 cucumber

Green Coco

As the Harry Nilsson and the Baha Men sing, "Put the lime in the coconut and drink them both up." Well, we can't resist adding some extra greens and a bit of lemon grass to create one of the most delicious ways to hydrate, alkalize, detox, and tantalize your taste buds. Close your eyes and you could be in Thailand.

1 pear (stalk removed)
1 cup kale
¼ lime (peel and pith removed)
1 lemon grass stalk
1 cucumber
¼ cup coconut water

Tropical Greens

Pineapple and greens are a win-win situation. Rich in vitamin C and antioxidants, this a great juice for any age, from eight to eighty, and it's also an excellent inflammation fighter for anyone suffering from arthritis.

4 cups kale | 3 cups broccoli (florets and stems) | 4 cups spinach | 2–3 celery sticks | 1½ cups skinned and chopped pineapple (with core)

Sweet Sexy Green

This fresh-tasting green juice is a DIY version of our best-selling cold-pressed juice. For a formidable list of alkalizing greens, the pear and basil give it a very balanced, easy-to-drink quality. This juice is my default juice of choice and will keep you buzzing all day.

½ head lettuce | 1½ pears (stalks removed) | 1 cup spinach | 1 cup kale | 4 broccoli florets and stems | ½ cup basil | 1 cucumber

Green and Orange

A sweet and sour green juice melody. The tartness of the pink grapefruit and the sweetness of the orange overpower the kale and spinach flavor. If you're new to greens, and a citrus lover, this is a great one to start with. Once you're used to the green flavors, we bet you'll want to graduate to greener pastures.

4 small carrots | 1 cup spinach | 1 cup kale | 1 orange (peeled) | 1 pink grapefruit (peel and pith removed) |

Expert tip

Remove peel and white pith from citrus fruits before juicing, as they are very bitter.

Detox in the City

The fennel and celery in this juice are extremely detoxifying for your digestive tract, and the entire cast of veg and fruits is filled with antioxidant and vitamin boosters. Just make sure your yellow pepper is ripe to maximize the vitamin C content.

4 large romaine lettuce leaves
½ yellow bell pepper (cored and seeded)
½ cup kale
1 tart green apple
1 sweet red apple
½ head fennel
4 celery sticks
1 cup spinach
1 in piece fresh ginger root (unpeeled)
¼ lemon (peel and pith removed)
½ cucumber

Watermelon Green Patch

This juice screams summer, and is very light, cooling, and refreshing. A wise choice if you are craving something sweet, but you get a bonus of a kale and cucumber salad in your glass!

½ cup fresh mint
1 cup kale
2 cups watermelon
    (skinned, seeded,
    and chopped)
1 cucumber

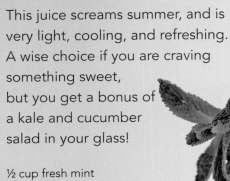

Expert tip

Use the white bits of watermelon closest to the skin. These contain high levels of flavonoids, lycopene, and vitamin C.

Green Glow-getter

Cilantro, fennel, and apple are an amazing base for this sweet and easy green juice. Our nutritional therapist Eve Kalinik (see page 12) designed this juice with skin health in mind — and after a few days of drinking this regularly, we have no doubt people will be noticing your glow!

1 cup broccoli pieces (florets and stems) | 1 cup fennel | 2 cups spinach | 2 apples (stalks removed) | ½ cup cilantro | 1 cup cucumber (chopped)

Brain-boosting Greens

This mild, sweet green juice is full of folate, which helps support your cognitive (smarty pants) function.

4 celery sticks | 2 pears (stalks removed) | 2 cups kale | 1in piece fresh ginger root (unpeeled) | 1 cup chard | 1 zucchini | ½ lime (peel and pith removed)

Drink Your Salad

This emerald-colored, slightly sweet juice is an amazing one to make in a large batch (because of the large list of ingredients), and decant into a few jam jars to drink over two days. Try this first thing in the morning, on an empty stomach, or as an afternoon snack.

2 apples (stalks removed) | ½ head romaine lettuce or green escarole | 1 cup kale | ½ cup parsley | 1 fresh green chile (seeded) | ¼ cup mint | ½ lime (peel and pith removed) | 1 large cucumber

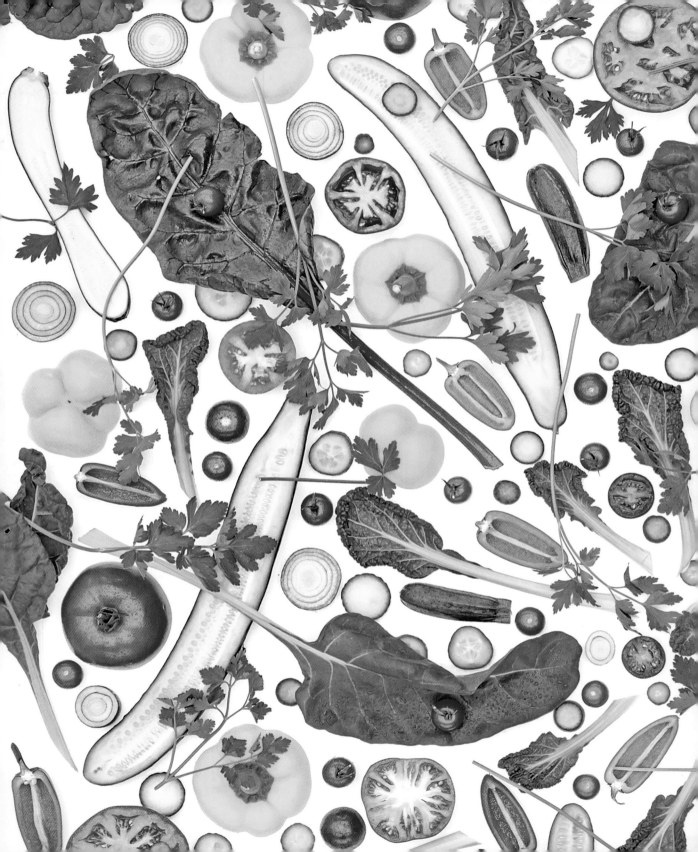

Hardcore Deep Greens

No fruits here

Mexican Mamacita

I desperately wanted to incorporate red onions into a juice, as I'm in love with their health benefits but don't love eating them raw. Onions are anti-inflammatory, antibacterial, and contain the phytochemical quercetin, which has been reported to help fight cancer. During recipe testing, we "high-fived" when we sampled this recipe, it's that good. Think gazpacho comes to the juice bar. I like this juice in the evening on a cleanse, as it's rather savory and a nice respite from sweeter juices I prefer during the day. You can keep the chile seeds in if you want some more heat. I do!

1 salad tomato | 1 green chile | 1 cup cilantro | ½ red onion (peeled) | 1½ cucumbers | ½ lime (peel and pith removed)

Rainbow Savory Dinner

This is a great intro to fruit-free vegetable juices. You'll be surprised how much sweetness the pepper and carrots contribute to the overall flavor, and the mildness of the cucumber and romaine lettuce really let it shine.

1 head romaine lettuce | ½ yellow or red bell pepper (cored and seeded) | ½ cup parsley | 4 carrots | ½ cucumber

Mellow Garden

Adding fresh herbs to your juices is a great trick for making even the most hardcore green juices super tasty and they are an excellent source of vitamin K and antioxidants. Try replacing an afternoon or late-night after-dinner coffee with this juice (with a splash of cherry juice) for a blissful night's sleep.

5 cups spinach | 4 cups romaine lettuce leaves | 5 cups kale | 3 cups broccoli pieces (florets and stems) | 1 cup parsley | 1 cup basil | 8 tbsp fresh lemon juice

Italian Savory Feast

We filed this under delicious "advanced" green juice. But be warned, it's not for the faint of heart or if you're brand new to green juices. The garlic packs a serious punch when combined with the basil. But don't be scared of garlic in your juice — it contains a hearty amount of sulfur compounds, which studies show promote healthy blood pressure levels. Mamma mia!

4 romaine lettuce leaves | 1 yellow bell pepper (cored and seeded) | 1 cup spinach | ½ cup fresh basil | ¼ red onion (peeled) | 1 garlic clove (peeled) | 1 cup cherry tomatoes | 1 zucchini

Fitness Fuel

Beets have been proven to increase stamina and power during workouts, helping you to exercise more efficiently. Mixed with a bit of kick from the ginger, and cucumber and greens, this is like an energy boost in a glass and is perfect for pre-exercise stamina.

2 cups beets (washed, trimmed, and chopped) | 2 cups kale | 2 cups spinach | 2in piece fresh ginger root (unpeeled) | 2 cups cucumber (chopped)

Spicy Beet Salad

The mix of sprouts, jalepeño, beets, and greens gives this juice a really interesting, complex flavor profile. If you don't like the earthiness of beet, this is a great one, as the other, strong flavors mellow it out. When you wash and prep all of the ingredients and see this huge salad before you that magically gets pressed into just one glass of juice, it's inspiring to visualize your nutrient intake in that single glass. I like a pinch of Himalayan salt for trace minerals and a savory taste.

2 beets (washed and trimmed) | 3–4 romaine lettuce leaves | ¼ cup alfafa sprouts | ¼ cup kale | 1in piece fresh ginger root (unpeeled) | ½ jalapeño chile (seeded) | ½ cucumber | ¼ lemon (peel and pith removed) | ¼ cup filtered water | pinch of Himalayan salt

Kale Mary ▶

This is a great virgin version of a Bloody Mary. Detoxifying and alkalizing greens aid in eliminating toxins, while fresh horseradish has a high level of glucosinolates, which help to detoxify the liver, as does apple cider vinegar. Kale Mary!

1 cup kale | 2 salad tomatoes | 3 celery sticks | 1 cucumber | 1 slice fresh horseradish root (unpeeled), about ½in thick (adjust according to how much kick you want) | pinch of cayenne pepper | dash of tamari | 1 tsp apple cider vinegar

Savory Green

Sugar snap peas are one of my favorite snacks because of their sweet taste, crisp texture, and vitamin-rich creds, and they add a surprisingly sweet flavor to this light, hydrating juice. I like drinking this juice after a run when I feel low on energy — the celery is full of rehydrating electrolytes, and the spiciness of the watercress and ginger wake me up.

3 celery sticks | ½ cup sugar snap peas (about 10) | ½ cup watercress | 1in piece fresh ginger root (unpeeled) | 1 cucumber | ½ lime (peel and pith removed) | pinch of cayenne pepper

Fruits

With veg, obviously!

Snake Charmer

Contributed by one of our experts, Romi Pulichino (see page 11), this recipe has been specially devised to help lift a flagging libido, and with the mix of watermelon and pomegranate, you'll find yourself transported in your mind to a terrace in Marrakesh. But be warned — even though it was created to, um, inspire your inner tiger, it's also wildly delicious, so be careful who you make it for!

2 celery sticks | 2 cups spinach | seeds of 1 pomegranate | 1½ cups watermelon (skinned, seeded, and chopped)

Fruity Pep

The hardest part about making this juice is not eating the raspberries before they get into your juicer! This juice is a gorgeous red color, and is both sweet and tart. Peppers are super high in antioxidant vitamin C and, with the addition of raspberries, it's chock-full of powerful phytonutrients. If you're drinking this because of Henrietta Norton's fertility advice (see pages 38–39), blend the juice with some avocado and maca for a luscious smoothie!

Juice the bell pepper and raspberries, run the wet pulp through the juicer again, and then juice the zucchini to wash the "bits" through.

1 red bell pepper (cored and seeded) | 1 cup raspberries | 2 zucchini | a squeeze of lime

FAB (Fennel, Apple, and Beet... and Friends)

This sweet and earthy juice is a FAB detoxifier. Whether you've had a big night, or feel a cold coming on, this juice will get you sorted. Beet, celery, and ginger are a great flavor combination and the fennel and fruits give it a strong sweetness. This is an excellent detox juice and diuretic, so make sure you follow this up with a glass of water!

1 pear (stalk removed) | 1 sweet apple such as Pink Lady, Jazz, or Braeburn (stalk removed) | 1 small beet (washed and trimmed) | ½ head fennel | 4 celery sticks | ½ head romaine lettuce | 1in piece fresh ginger root (unpeeled)

Thai Melon Brightener ▶

I love this juice in summer for an instant cooler and vitamin hit, and in the dead of winter to lift my mood when there is no sunny vacation in sight! It's a very light juice, not "heavy'" enough for a cleanse but a great antioxidant, carotene-boosting snack.

½ cantaloupe (or gaia) melon (skinned and seeded) | 1½ cucumbers | 1 lemon grass stalk | ¼ cup cilantro | ¼ cup coconut water

Pineapple Power

Wheatgrass. Some love the taste, some don't. Even after years of drinking wheatgrass shots, I admit that it isn't my favorite flavor, but it does make me buzz like an espresso. Wheatgrass is one of nature's most effective healers because of the chlorophyll content (see page 20) and its A, B-complex, C, E, and K vitamins, plus the handy fact that it contains heaps of amino acids, the building blocks of protein. Here, I've mixed wheatgrass juice (or powder if you can't find the fresh stuff) with sweet, tangy pineapple, which turns any drinking experience into a tropical treat.

1 cup wheatgrass (about ¼ tray of wheatgrass, cut just before soil level) or 1 tsp wheatgrass powder plus ¼ cup water | 2 cups skinned and chopped pineapple (with core)

Expert tip

Juice the wheatgrass first, followed by the pineapple to wash through the wheatgrass. Drink immediately.

Spicy Limonade

This is a DIY version of our cold-pressed Spicy Limonade. Depending on the power of your juicer, you may need as much as 2–3 chiles to get a dollop of juice from them. Our Spicy Limonade in the cold-pressed range only has ½ chile, but the powerful cold press extracts a significant amount of brightly colored juice as compared to a home juicer, so fear not if the color of your limonade is a more mellow color than the branded PLENISH juices. With more vitamin C than an orange, lemons, and limes are a great immunity booster, and the chiles will revvvv your metabolism.

1 lemon (peel and pith removed) | ½ lime (peel and pith removed) | 1–2 red chiles (seeded) | 1 tbsp agave nectar | 1⅔ cups filtered water

Expert tip

This is a cleansing staple, but also makes a great coffee substitute in the afternoon.

🌀 Stress Buster

With a base of kiwi fruit and orange, it tastes more fruit than veg, but don't be fooled — 2 cups each of chard and celery sneak in a "salad" to create a nutritionally dense powerhouse. Kiwis are a natural source of serotonin, which has a calming effect on the body, and the high levels of vitamin C in the oranges help regulate cortisol levels (the hormone produced by the adrenals when stressed). Finally, the celery contains a category of phytonutrients called phthalides, which can have a sedative effect on the body. If you are stressed and find yourself reaching for candy or another unhealthy comfort food, try this juice first — it's healthier and the after-effects will help rather than exacerbate the issue at hand.

2 cups chard | 2 celery sticks | 3 kiwi fruit (peeled) | 2 oranges (peeled)

Expert tip

Chop the chard finely before juicing and juice first, as it can get stuck in the juicer.

Minty Apple

It's hard not to like this juice. We dare you to find a child who doesn't like it either! With its pink color and sweet taste, it's quite an easy way to deliver kids (or veg juice newbies) a large serving of green veggies and herbs.

2 apples | 4 celery sticks | ½ cup mint | 1 cup strawberries (hulled)

Strawberry Rhubarb Tart ▶

This is a tart and sweet juice, with a unique, indulgent flavor thanks to the anti-inflammatory cinnamon. I often make this for "dessert" at brunch and it's always a conversation piece.

1 zucchini | 4 rhubarb stalks | 2 apples (stalks removed) | ½ cup strawberries (hulled) | ½ tsp ground cinnamon

Black and Blue Salad

This is a delicious, sweet, and easy lazy-morning juice, with only two ingredients to wash and put through the juicer. Blueberries and spinach are two of the most powerful antioxidants in the plant kingdom, so are a power duo in this juice.

½ cup blueberries | 1 apple (stalk and core removed) | 1 cup spinach | ½ cup coconut water

Expert tip

Reserve some coconut water to run through the juicer last to unstick the blueberries and spinach.

Ginger PAM (Pineapple, Apple, and Mint)

This instant refresher is our own little fountain of youth. A source of vitamin A, Ginger PAM helps maintain healthy skin and hair, and the large dose of vitamin C (the super antioxidant) in it also provides help to support your immune system and prevent cells from oxidative stress (because what's the point of looking good, if you're not feeling good?). This is an ode to Pineapple Squared in the PLENISH cold-pressed range, but I've added a bit of fresh ginger for an extra detox benefit and, well, it just tastes marvelous, dahling!

1 red apple (stalk removed)

1 tart green apple (stalk removed)

1in piece fresh ginger root (unpeeled)

¼ cup fresh mint

2 cups skinned and chopped pineapple (with core)

⏱ Craving Killa'

Trying to lose weight or find healthy alternatives to sweet treats? This is a great fresh-tasting, juicy smoothie for any time of the day. Grapefruit contributes to the breakdown of fat in the body, while the oleic acid (a monounsaturated fatty acid) in the avocado keeps you feeling satisfied and your blood sugar levels balanced.

Juice the broccoli, grapefruits, and carrots then blend with the avocado.

4–5 broccoli florets and stems | 2 pink grapefruit (peel and pith removed) | 2 carrots | ½ avocado (pitted, skinned, and coarsely chopped)

Expert tip

You can't juice avocado so add to a blender, along with the juiced ingredients, and blend until smooth.

Ginger CAM (Cucumber, Apple, and Mint)

Meet Ginger PAM's (see opposite) super sister. With high levels of antioxidants in fresh apple juice, and B vitamins and electrolytes in cucumber to replenish many essential nutrients, this green lady is fresh and tasty.

2 sweet apples (stalks removed) | ½in piece fresh ginger root (unpeeled) | ¼ cup mint | 1 cucumber

Self-tanner

Vibrant and orange in color, resist the urge to lather this juice on your body! Super high in carotenes (the phytonutrients that make the melon, carrot, and pepper orange) that not only protect your cells from oxidative stress but can help give your skin a healthy glow.

3 carrots | 1 orange bell pepper (cored and seeded) | ½ cantaloupe melon (skinned and seeded)

Cholesterol Police

Apple, carrot, and basil are the strong flavors in this "bad" cholesterol-fighting juice created by Dr. Nigma Talib (see page 13). The sweetness of the carrots and the tang of the green apples create a really smooth, well-balanced juice. Turmeric can add a bit more heat to the flavor, so start with a small pinch and work your way up as your taste for it develops.

Expert tip

For a superfood booster, blend the ingredients with 1 tsp unprocessed virgin coconut oil.

3 carrots | 1 cup basil | 1 cup spinach | 2 Granny Smith apples (stalks removed) | pinch of ground turmeric

Greens and Grapes

I'm a big fan of ginger shots when I feel like I'm coming down with something, although they do make you feel like your head will explode (albeit in a good way), and on a recent trip to California I tried a ginger and grape shot, which inspired this juice. While the ginger and grape flavors are out in front, the cucumber and pear work to mellow out that ginger hit, so it's a real joy to drink. Grapes contain the phytonutrients polyphenols, for which there is evidence of cancer-protective properties, and the ginger is a powerful antibacterial, so a good pick-me-up if you're feeling run-down.

1 pear (stalk removed) | 2 cups kale | 1 cup green grapes | 1in piece fresh ginger root (unpeeled) | 1½ cucumbers

◀ Smooth Move

If you live in a big city, papaya is likely to be reminiscent of a tropical vacation, so that's a good start. And this papaya, carrot and lime combo is simply happiness in a glass, the spinach adding a shot of freshness and cutting the sweetness a bit. Speaking of vacations, we know traveling can lead to constipation, and this is a magical elixir designed by nutritional therapist Gabriela Peacock (see page 12) to help get your digestive system moving if you are backed up.

½ papaya (peeled and seeded) | 2 apples (stalks removed) | 4 carrots | 2 cups spinach | ¼ lime (peel and pith removed)

Turmeric Tonic

This is a tart and sweet anti-inflammatory and immunity-boosting juice. Juice the fruit and herbs, mix with the water, and then add the turmeric to your taste — start with a small pinch, and work your way up to a ½ teaspoon. The turmeric will completely change the vivid green color, but fear not. Because of the natural preservative levels of orange and lemon juice, it will last three to four days in the fridge.

1 orange (peeled) | ½ lemon (peel and pith removed) | ¼ cup parsley | ¾ cup water | ground turmeric to taste

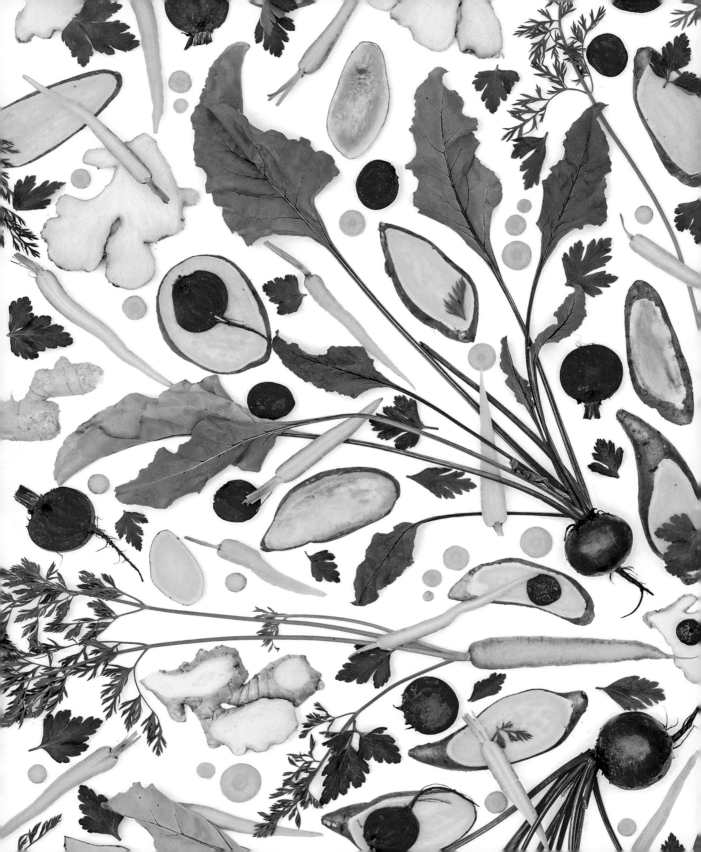

Roots

With fruits and greens

Yamapple

A DIY version of the Sweet Potato Pie in the PLENISH cold-pressed range. Although it tastes like a naughty sweet potato pie, this provides a healthy dose of vitamins A and C; in fact your entire Recommended Dietary Allowance (RDA) in one glass! It's also incredibly satisfying and can be used as a meal replacement.

2 sweet potatoes
3 apples (stalks removed)
½ tsp ground cinnamon
pinch of ground nutmeg

🍷 Liver Supporter

This is a serious detox juice. With six beets juiced into one glass along with a hearty portion of kale, your liver will thank you for all of the detox support. I've said it before and I'll say it again: don't chug beet juice. Drink it slowly, and chew your juice.

6 beets (washed and trimmed) | 3 cups kale | 4 carrots | ¼ lemon (peel and pith removed)

Carotene Cuties

A lighter version of Yamapple (see opposite), this juice is an ode to beta-carotene, chock-full of vitamins A and C for immunity support, and a great antioxidant boost.

2 sweet potatoes | 4 carrots | ½ cantaloupe melon (skinned and seeded)

Beetbox

This is designed for the ultimate beet lover. It has an intense beet flavor and you should drink it slowly, as beet juice is a very potent detoxifier, so chugging it could make you feel ill. Don't fear if your trips to the bathroom are a little more red/pink for a day or two; just sayin'.

2 small beets (washed and trimmed) | 4 carrots | ¼ lime (peel and pith removed) | 1in piece fresh ginger root (unpeeled) | ¼ cup water or pomegranate juice

◀ 👣 G*Out* Getter

This is a slightly greener version of the Cherry Beets in the PLENISH cold-pressed range that has been tweaked to aid clients suffering from gout. It doesn't hurt that the beet–cherry combo is wildly delish, or that it's extremely alkalizing and a mild diuretic. Whether you're treating gout or a heavy night, this should be on your "regulars" list. Push all the ingredients, except the lemon juice, through the juicer. Then run the juice through twice more to remove more of the pulp. Add the lemon juice once finished.

1½ cups pitted cherries | 1 beet (washed and trimmed) | 2 cups romaine lettuce leaves | 2 cups chopped celery | 2 tbsp fresh lemon juice

Purple CAG (Cabbage, Apple, and Ginger)

We eat purple cabbage in my house often and I wanted to do a play on the UK favorite Carrot, Apple, and Ginger. This juice has a gorgeous purple color, and a bit of a kick to it, too, but the apple and cinnamon give it a really indulgent, sophisticated flavor.

⅛ head small purple cabbage | 4 carrots | 2 apples (stalks removed) | 1in piece fresh ginger root (unpeeled) | ½ tsp ground cinnamon

Hypertension Hero ♡ ▶

This just tastes good for you! Another contribution from Dr. Nigma (see page 13), this time to help reduce blood pressure, this juice is a powerhouse of celery, beet, and broccoli flavors, but the apple and parsley give it a very fresh lift. We give it a 180 over 60!

5 celery sticks | 1 beet (washed and trimmed) | 3 broccoli florets and stems | 2 cups spinach | ¼ cup parsley | 2 apples (stalks removed)

Clean Roots

A lighter, less beety version of Beetbox (see page 97), this is a sweet and fresh juice, and great for energy and cardiovascular health.

1 beet (washed and trimmed) | 2 carrots | 2 cups spinach | 2 small apples (stalks removed) | ¼ lemon (peel and pith removed)

Nutm*lks

Everything but the cow

Moo Who?

Nutm*lks are a great way to reduce or eliminate the amount of dairy products in your life and can be consumed plain on their own, or used in tea and coffee, on cereal or anywhere you would use regular milk.

*cashew m*lk, see opposite*

*cacao cashew m*lk, see page 106*

Cashew M*lk

Thick and Creamy

I like my cashew m*lk quite creamy, so I use a 2:5 cashew to water ratio, as follows:

⅔ cup raw cashew nuts | 1⅔ cups water | seeds scraped from ½ vanilla bean | 2 dates (pitted) | pinch of ground Himalayan salt

Soak the cashews in the water for at least 2 hours. Add to a blender along with the remaining ingredients and blend until smooth. Refrigerate immediately and serve ice cold.

Thin and M*lky

If you prefer your cashew m*lk more of a skim m*lk consistency, blend the cashews and water together, strain through cheesecloth, squeezing out all the liquid, and discard the pulp. Rinse out the blender, add the strained nutm*lk and the other ingredients, and blend until smooth.

*almond m*lk, see page 107*

Expert tip

When straining, wet the cheesecloth so that it sticks to the sides of the jar or cup to help prevent spillage.

105

Alkaline Iced Coffee

This is a great alkaline, caffeine-free version of an iced coffee.

2 cups Cashew M*lk (see page 105) | 1 tsp ground roasted chicory

Blend together in a blender until there are no visual chicory granules, then refrigerate immediately. Serve ice cold.

Cacao Cashew M*lk

Cacao (or chocolate) cashew m*lk needs little introduction, so just try it. Everyone who has done so loved it so much that I decided to launch it in the PLENISH cold-pressed range. Warning: this won't last long!

2 cups Cashew M*lk (see page 105) | 2 tsp cacao powder | 1 date (pitted)

Blend together in a blender until the cacao and date are fully liquidized, then refrigerate immediately. Serve ice cold.

Almond M*lk

The addition of dates makes this nutm*lk ultra-delish, and also contributes a bit of fiber and sweetness.

²/₃ cup blanched almonds | 1²/₃cups water | 2 dates (pitted)

Soak the almonds in the water overnight, then blend in a blender until smooth. Strain through cheesecloth, squeezing out all of the liquid, and discard the pulp. Rinse out the blender, add the strained nutm*lk and dates, and blend until smooth. Refrigerate immediately and serve ice cold.

If you only have whole raw almonds, don't panic. You can use them to make your m*lk, you just might find that the consistency is not quite as smooth and the color is darker due to the flecks of skin.

Alternatively, blanch your almonds by soaking them in very hot water for about 10–15 minutes (or until the water has cooled). This will loosen the skin from around each nut. Drain, then squeeze each almond between your thumb and forefinger. You will find the nuts slide easily from their skins. *Et Voilà!* Blanched almonds ready for soaking and blending.

Expert tip

If you're trying to keep your sugar levels low, omit the dates. It's still divine!

Once Upon a Cleanse

A very wise and muscular client (and now friend of mine) is a widely loved personal trainer called Matt Miller and not a stranger to various cleanses. When he signed up for his first PLENISH cleanse, he said he was in need of a service, and I thought this was a brilliant analogy. The truth is, most people think about the inner workings of their car more often than their own bodies. This is exactly what a cleanse is designed to do.

What is a Cleanse?

The best things in life happen at the edge of your comfort zone

A cleanse is a check-in with your body and mind to assess how you are feeling, how efficient your body is working, and to help pinpoint any areas that you may be able to improve with simple changes to your diet. Eating and drinking can be a very emotional response to dealing with stress and everyday life. When we remove the element of common comforts (candy, bread, booze, multiple coffees) from our daily routines, we are forced to evaluate how much we depend on these consumptions. As much as a cleanse is designed to detoxify your physical body, it can also be very emotionally cleansing, giving you the opportunity to start working on any emotional issues that you may have around food.

In the purely physical sense, a cleanse is a healthy form of routine maintenance that provides your digestive system and liver with the rest they need in order to release accumulated toxins. At the same time, you will be flooding your system with organic, easy-to-digest liquid nutrition filled with living enzymes and vitamins. By increasing the organic and raw green juices you consume while eliminating refined sugars, coffee, alcohol, meat, and too much cooked food, you will shift your body to a more oxygen-drenched alkaline system (see pages 17–19), which will reduce inflammation, boost immunity, promote good health, and help prevent any chronic "dis-eases."

Doesn't the body detox itself?

As we discussed in The Knowledge (see pages 14–25), the digestive system, liver, skin, and lymphatic system are a great cleaning crew that removes the toxins we consume. The problem is that in today's society, we often get in the way of our internal detoxification systems by overloading them with toxins from unclean water, medications, supplements, alcohol, stimulants like coffee and tea, pesticides and hormones from non-organic foods, home-cleaning chemicals, environmental pollutants, and heavy metals. The body's detoxification systems get overloaded and, like your car, need a good clear-out and an overhaul.

How long should I cleanse for?

This is a very personal decision. If you have never cleansed before, you may want to start with a three-day cleanse and work your way up to a five- to seven-day cleanse. That being said, if you already live a nearly raw, vegan lifestyle or have cleansed before, five days may be an easy starting point for you. A five-day cleanse is 60 percent more cleansing time than a three-day cleanse, and you will release that many more toxins. It's like deciding how long a vacation you should take, either a long weekend or an extended break, based on how you are feeling.

Which level is right for me?

If you've never cleansed before, you can start with Level 1 (Beginner) and graduate through the levels as you gain more confidence. As you progress up the levels toward Level 3 (Advanced), you will consume more green than fruit and root juices.

A cleanse may benefit you if you:

- Regularly feel bloated or puffy after eating
- Have candida
- Find your skin has lost its glow
- Are low on energy and fatigued
- Have trouble sleeping
- Have joint pain or stiffness
- Have a few stubborn pounds to lose
- Are feeling mentally foggy
- Need a hard stop from a period of overindulgence

Expert tip

If you are sensitive to sugar, have candida, or are looking for the most alkaline option (see pages 17–19), try Level 3, which is mostly green juices. Choose from Sweet and Easy Greens (see pages 62–69), which contain some fruit, or Hardcore Deep Greens (see pages 70–77), all without fruit.

A cautionary note

These cleanses are designed to be undertaken during your everyday life. If you are pregnant, have an eating disorder, or a compromised immune system, a cleanse is not right for you. We do not recommend cleansing for longer than seven days unless you are supervised by a medical professional, or are attending a facility designed to oversee extended cleanses. Please consult a medical practitioner before undertaking any new diet program or if you have any health considerations.

The Cleanse Program

Ready to reboot

Whatever it is that made you pick up this book and embark on a healthier way of eating, bravo! You've made the essential first step (the hardest one) to call a halt to any habits or symptoms that you are uncomfortable with. You are ready to hit CTRL + ALT + DELETE, reboot your health and turn over a new green leaf. We are all a work in progress emotionally and physically, so each cleanse can be used to focus on small but impactful changes you'd like to make.

Over the following pages, play close attention to the Pre-cleanse Prep (see page 116) and The PLENISH Pantry Makeover (see pages 114–115), which will play a huge part in your success before you even start your cleanse. While detox is meant to be a "reset button," you do need to clear the decks before your cleanse to make the most of your commitment.

We've put together three different levels of juice cleanse: Level 1 — Beginner; Level 2 — Intermediate; Level 3 — Advanced. For all three levels, the three days of pre-cleanse and three days of post-cleanse (see page 120) are essential parts of the entire cleanse process.

The schedule countdown

4 days pre-cleanse	Give your kitchen a PLENISH Pantry Makeover (see pages 114–115) and start eliminating foods from your Foods to Lose list.
3 days pre-cleanse	Embark on your Pre-cleanse Prep (see page 116).
2 days pre-cleanse	Choose your level (see table opposite). Shop for produce using the Foods to Choose list (see page 115) and Juice Recipes (see pages 62–107). Stock up on extra lemons and herbal teas to accompany your cleanse.
1 day pre-cleanse	Make your juices for the following day. Get into the habit of doing this each day throughout your cleanse: having your juices ready for the day ahead means no excuses.

The cleanse levels

- Each level is based on six juices per day.
- The difference in level is based on the amount of green juice versus fruit and root juice you consume on the schedule.
- You will always start with a nutrient-dense green juice in the morning, when your system is primed to assimilate all of the chlorophyll and phytonutrients to energize you and boost detoxification. Warning: it may make you buzz, akin to coffee!
- Cashew M*lk is suggested as your sixth and last juice of the day. It's very filling and will prevent you from being hungry in the evening. There is a significant amount of magnesium in cashew nuts, which will help regulate your sleep, although please try to finish your m*lk at least two hours before bed.
- The Spicy Limonade in each level is there to keep your metabolism revving, boost immunity and give your system an alkaliZING each day. It's also a nice break from the vegetable and fruit juices.
- *On Level 3, we suggest choosing at least two green juices from Hardcore Deep Greens (see pages 70–77), which contain no fruit.

	Level 1—Beginner	Level 2—Intermediate	Level 3*—Advanced
1	Green juice (see pages 62–77)	Green juice (see pages 62–77)	Green juice* (see pages 70–77)
2	Fruit juice (see pages 78–93)	Fruit juice (see pages 78–93)	Green juice (see pages 62–77)
3	Green juice (see pages 62–77)	Green juice (see pages 62–77)	Green juice (see pages 62–77)
4	Spicy Limonade (see page 84)	Spicy Limonade (see page 84)	Spicy Limonade (see page 84)
5	Root juice (see pages 94–101)	Green juice (see pages 62–77)	Green juice* (see pages 70–77)
6	Cashew M*lk (see page 105)	Cashew M*lk (see page 105)	Cashew M*lk (see page 105)

The PLENISH Pantry Makeover

A cleanse can reset your way of eating and create a clean slate on which to build a new healthy foundation. We highly recommend cleansing your kitchen before you cleanse your body. This will make sure the foods that tempted you in the past are not around during your cleanse and that post-cleanse you have all the "clean" ingredients on hand to allow you to prepare nutritious, healthy meals.

Start as you wish to continue

Our food choices can often be a case of pure convenience and not having the right ingredients available to make more nutritious dishes. Having a well-curated pantry of healthy essentials will assure you have everything ready for your pre- and post-cleanse menus, but will also set your intentions (and your kitchen) for a healthier way of life after the cleanse itself.

I've put together a shopping list to help you detox your pantry and PLENISH it with the right foods (and a list of which ones to phase out).

Foods to lose

- **White foods** (except cauliflower!) including white, refined carbohydrates such as bread, pasta, rice, chips, and noodles.
- **Sugar** in all its glorious guises including candy, chocolate, cakes, and cookies.
- **Dairy products** including milk, cheese (all types), yogurt, cream, and ice cream.
- **Processed soy products** including soy milk, soy yogurts, soy desserts, and processed meat-free foods.
- **Alcohol** in any form.
- **Caffeine** found in coffee and teas.
- **Yeasts** found in bread, cakes, and cheese.
- **Processed foods and ready meals**, i.e. anything that comes in a bag or box — if you can't pronounce or recognize any ingredient they contain, lose it!

Foods to choose

Fresh veggies and plenty of them! Go for the rainbow with a mix of vibrant colors — kale, broccoli, arugula, watercress, spinach, chard, endive, beet, sweet potatoes, fennel, cucumber… you get the idea.

- **Fresh garlic** for its hero health benefits and to add plenty of flavor.
- **Dates** for sweetening.
- **Himalayan salt or sea salt** for its mineral content.
- **Ground chicory** as a coffee substitute.
- **Herbal teas** in plenty.
- **Delicious dressing ingredients** for salad and veggies including tamari (a gluten-free soy sauce), cider vinegar, lemons, mirin, and miso paste.
- **Gluten-free grains** including quinoa, amaranth, gluten-free oats, buckwheat, millet, and brown rice.
- **Nutm*lks** such as cashew or almond (see pages 105–107 for homemade) instead of cows' milk.
- **Coconut yogurt** to replace dairy or soy versions.
- **Nutritional yeast** to give a non-dairy cheese taste to dishes.
- **Healthy oils** such as olive, sesame, walnut, pumpkin are great for their anti-inflammatory properties. But just don't heat these guys, as it damages their structure and reverses their health-giving properties. Instead, cook with coconut oil, which is solid at room temperature.
- **Good fats** found in nuts and seeds, avocados, oily fish, and organic free-range eggs. Make sure your nuts and seeds are raw (unroasted and unsalted) and have a nice selection of nut/ seed butters on hand — cashew, almond, and sesame (tahini) butters are staples in the PLENISH pantry. Fats are super important in the diet to help support healthy and strong cell membranes and to provide anti-inflammatory benefits. Did you know that on average just two Brazil nuts provide you with your daily intake of selenium, an important antioxidant mineral that supports thyroid hormone metabolism?
- **Legumes** such as Puy and red lentils, lima beans and chickpeas. Buy them dried, soak if necessary (in the case of beans and chickpeas — follow the pack instructions) and cook up in a big batch so that you can freeze.
- **Spices and herbs**, fresh or dried, can transform a simple dish and have a host of nutritional benefits. These include paprika, cayenne pepper, turmeric, cinnamon, red pepper flakes, oregano, sage, cumin, rosemary, thyme, and vanilla beans.

Start Your Pre-cleanse Program

So you've set the date and now it's the big countdown to cleansing! The key to success when embarking on any new healthy regime is preparation, preparation, and preparation. The more you can do before Day 1 of the cleanse, the better you are going to feel during and after the cleanse itself. Having a huge supper or rosé binge the day before is not going to make you feel good. Trust us.

Pre-cleanse prep

Tidy up for a deep clean

Think of your pre-cleanse prep as tidying up before your house cleaner comes. There is no point in hiring a deep cleaner if you can't get to the floor! Your pre-cleanse eating plan will start sweeping out your system, so when you start cleansing, you'll be able to dig a little deeper than the burger you ate 48 hours ago and properly allow your body to detox.

Options to lose

For at least three days before your cleanse, really start to clean up your diet, eliminating all acidic and heavy foods including sugar, meat, coffee, caffeinated teas, carbonated drinks, dairy, alcohol, and refined or processed foods.

Options to choose

Instead, heap your plate up with plenty of fresh raw or lightly steamed vegetables, avocados, salad, fruits, and raw nuts and seeds. The more you do to ensure a smooth transition into the cleanse, the easier and more beneficial your experience will be and the less you will suffer from unpleasant detox symptoms.

Pre-cleanse menu

To get you inspired, we have put together a delicious plant-based pre-cleanse menu and recipe plan for you to follow. Feel free to swap the meals around, or if you are pressed for time, make a big batch of one dish and eat it over one to three days. The last day before your cleanse should be the lightest eating day, as we've outlined below.

Three days to go	Two days to go	One day to go
Breakfast: Raw Buckwheat Porridge (see page 124)	**Breakfast:** Apple and Ginger Bircher Muesli (see page 123)	**Breakfast:** Cinnamon-spiced Pineapple with Coconut Yogurt (see page 123)
Lunch: Avocado, Radish, and Spinach Quinoa Salad (see page 129)	**Lunch:** Sesame Sweet Potato and Kale with Tahini Dressing (see page 127)	**Lunch:** Ultimate Leafy Greens (see page 127)
Dinner: Celeriac, Wilted Chard, and Hazelnut Lentils (see page 135)	**Dinner:** Moroccan Spicy Carrots and Beets with Paprika Hummus (see page 133)	**Dinner:** Broccoli and Almond Soup (see page 135)

Hot water and lemon

This is a very easy ritual we hope you will continue for the rest of your long, healthy life — it's that impactful. Start each morning with a mug of warm or hot water and with the juice of half a lemon squeezed in. These are just a few of the superpowers of this easy, magical elixir:

- Wakes up your digestive system by encouraging peristalsis, the involuntary contractions of the intestine, which gets things moving.
- Boosts your immune system because lemons are high in vitamin C and are antibacterial.
- Promotes clear skin by speeding up detoxification and eliminating the toxins that cause blemishes.
- Helps create an alkaline pH, which is essential for good health (see pages 17–19).

Expert tip

If you're a heavy coffee drinker, to avoid a major headache, phase out the coffee slowly in the week leading up to your cleanse. Try half decaf/half regular on Day 1, green tea on Day 2, and cut it completely on Day 3 before your cleanse. If you are suffering caffeine-withdrawal headaches, have some green tea or matcha alongside your cleanse until it subsides.

It's Cleanse Day!

Whether you're working or have limited time during the day, we highly recommend that you make a full day's cleanse the evening before, and store the juices in jam jars or airtight bottles. This allows you to stay on track if any unexpected obstacles crop up in your day (a missed alarm clock, surprise meeting, or a long night with a crying child). You get my point — create a well-prepared plan so there can be no excuses!

Rise and shine

Upon waking, have some hot water and lemon (see page 117) to wake up and alkalize your system. Give yourself a dry brush, have a good stretch (and maybe meditate!) and thank yourself for the commitment you've made to your health over the next few days.

Timing

Drink your six juices in their numbered order as often as you need to. It may help to number them the night before so that you don't need to think during a busy day. There is no strict schedule, but a good rule of thumb is to wait at least one hour between juices and to finish the cashew m*lk at least two hours before you sleep.

Hydrate and elminate

Drink as much water and herbal tea as you can throughout the day. This will amplify your cleanse benefits and enhance your energy levels. If you're having tummy trouble, read Gabriela Peacock's tips on busting constipation (see pages 28–29), or try a colonic cleansing treatment through a licensed practitioner.

Move it!

Our clients commonly ask if they can exercise on a cleanse. It's OK and recommended to keep up some level of physical activity. Listen to your body to see what kind and intensity of movement feels good. A brisk walk can be a great fatigue buster, or if you wake up feeling full of beans, push yourself a bit harder. We do not recommend extended high-intensity workouts, but if you are He-Man, who are we to stop you? You just may want to have a little of your nutm*lk before or after your workout (or perhaps a whole extra one!).

Cleanse your social plans

If your week usually has work or social engagements that take place at restaurants and bars, we highly recommend scheduling your cleanse during a time when you can block off a few days without these activities. For friends, suggest a walk, run, yoga class, or massage/spa appointment instead of a restaurant/bar catch-up. If you have a work engagement, bring your juice and be a conversation starter. Worst-case scenario if the peer pressure becomes too much to enjoy your emerald green liquid lunch? Order a mixed green salad (no cheese or meat) and just have some lemon juice and olive oil drizzled over it.

Extra credit

Embrace your cleanse period as a time to nourish and pamper yourself. You've already committed to nourishing and detoxifying your cells, so why not book in a treatment or home-based treat to help fill the time that was once consumed by eating, make you feel good, and amplify your detoxification? Here's a few suggestions:

- A lymphatic drainage massage
- An extra nap — the laundry can wait
- A meditation or stretching class
- Dry brush your skin (dry brushes are available at most pharmacies or online) to reveal brighter, glowing skin, help the body eliminate toxins, promote blood circulation, and reduce the visibility of cellulite (yes please!).

The cheat sheet

Although we recommend abstaining from eating solid food for the duration of your cleanse, we recognize that this can be difficult, particularly if you've never done it before. If you're starting to feel uncomfortable, or have any other unpleasant symptoms, don't beat yourself up. Instead, congratulate yourself on what you have accomplished, even if it's only a half day. If you stop earlier than planned, simply have your goal in mind for your next cleanse (remember, we are all a work in progress). The best thing you can do is listen to your body. Try a hot water with lemon (see page 117) or a green tea, as this can sometimes be enough to stave off the need for solid food. If this is not enough, make some sensible choices from our recommendations below:

- 1 cup pureed broccoli
- 1 cup cucumber slices
- ¼ avocado (pitted and skinned)
- 2 celery sticks
- 1 cup cashew or almond nutm*lk (see pages 105 and 107)
- 1 cup shredded kale or lettuce with lemon juice

Post-cleanse

Hurrah! You've nearly made it to the last day and feeling ready to take on the world with a renewed sense of vigor and gusto. A reminder that your cleanse ends the morning after your final juice, so no victory dinner or champagne after your last nutm*lk — we want to help your digestive system wake up GENTLY and SLOWLY! Use your common sense when introducing solids, especially meat, dairy, and alcohol. Your body is your best guide, so listen to it.

The clean slate and post-cleanse wave

Sometimes the thought of eating solid food can be almost anticlimatic, but think about breaking your cleanse as an opportunity to ride that post-cleanse wave and reset your eating patterns for life. You may be surprised that the indulgences you were craving last week are not the first thing you are looking forward to eating. You are embarking on life with a clean slate with newly sensitized taste buds, and post-cleanse is the perfect time to build a healthy, strong foundation based on clean, nutrient-dense foods. Now where is that green juice?

The morning after and beyond

Starting the morning after your last juice, introduce light foods such as fruits and vegetables and little of the more dense rice, potatoes, and breads. We want to start your digestive system slowly and gently, and nausea is never a welcome return to solid food. Foods such as meat, dairy, caffeine, and alcohol should not be introduced until at least seven days after the cleanse (if ever!). We highly recommend introducing one of these eliminated food groups one by one every other day to see how they affect how you feel. Listen to your body and it will tell you if it's unhappy! For example, if you reintroduce grains and feel fine but two days later you introduce yogurt and get bloated and gassy, then maybe your system does better without that food group.

A few questions to ask yourself as you reintroduce solid foods:

- How does it feel to chew your first meal? After coming off solids, notice how you want to chew more to liquefy your foods, making it easier on your stomach and intestines to digest what's coming.
- As you reintroduce grains, or even meat and dairy (if necessary), how do you feel directly after eating those foods? Lack of energy? Bloating?

Post-cleanse menu

Here's our post-cleanse menu to get you securely on the path of lifelong healthier eating and to really reap the benefits of the cleanse itself.

Post-cleanse Day 1	Post-cleanse Day 2	Post-cleanse Day 3
Breakfast: Super Greens Smoothie Bowl (see page 124)	**Breakfast**: Portobello Stack (see page 126)	**Breakfast**: Gluten-free Granola (see page 126)
Lunch: Cauliflower Tabbouleh (see page 130)	**Lunch**: Rainbow Slaw (see page 130)	**Lunch**: Avocado, Kale, and Hemp Hearts Salad (see page 129)
Dinner: Zucchinetti with Cashew Pesto (see page 137)	**Dinner**: Miso Sesame Carrots and Leeks with Black Beans (see page 137)	**Dinner**: Roasted Red Pepper and Lima Bean Quinoa Salad (see page 134)

Cleanse Symptoms

Normal symptoms	Suggestion
Headache	Stick it out for 24 hours, or have a cup of green tea. If you are a committed coffee drinker, going cold turkey without caffeine can bring on headaches and the low levels of caffeine in green tea will help. Drink lots of water too.
Nausea	Drink more water to speed up the elimination of toxins. Drink your juices slowly, and chew them well. Nausea can be an unwelcome side-effect of drinking beet too fast.
Feeling cold	Drink hot herbal teas throughout the day.
Diarrhea	You want it out, so let it out! It will subside when you get old matter out of your colon. Did you know that many of us carry between 2–15lb of waste in our colon? It's gotta come out!
Constipation	See pages 28–29.
Fogginess/Lack of concentration	You can feel slightly hazy on Days 1 and 2, but you will see the light as soon as the bulk of what you've been holding on to has been eliminated. Water will help to accelerate this process. Hang in there!
Growling stomach	You're ready for your next juice. Make sure you're drinking a tall glass of water between each juice. A hot herbal tea can help ward off hunger too.
Fatigue	Your body is working hard. If you're tired, take a nap and make sure you are getting to bed at least two hours earlier than usual.

Abnormal symptoms	Suggestion
Vomiting	If you have NOT had a beet-based juice, stop juicing and drink water, then have some avocado or a banana. Call your doctor if you are not feeling better immediately.
Bloody poop	It's common for beet to turn your feces and urine red, and can happen over 12 hours after consumption. This is not a concern. If you have not consumed beet juice, contact your doctor.

Apple and Ginger Bircher Muesli

Serves 1

⅔ cup gluten-free oats | 1 cup Cashew M*lk (see page 105) or Almond M*lk (see page 107) plus a little extra if needed | 2 tbsp chia seeds | dash of fresh lemon juice | seeds scraped from ½ vanilla bean or ¼ tsp vanilla powder | ¼ tsp ground ginger | thinly sliced apple to serve

Mix all the ingredients, except the apple, together in a glass jar or bowl, cover and place in the fridge overnight.

In the morning, remove from the fridge and let stand for 10 minutes at room temperature before adding a little additional m*lk if needed. Serve with a few thin slices of apple.

Cinnamon-spiced Pineapple with Coconut Yogurt

Serves 1

1 generous handful of skinned, cored, and 1in diced pineapple | ½ tsp ground cinnamon | pinch of mild chili powder | ½ cup dairy-free coconut milk yogurt and a squeeze of lime juice to serve

Pop the pineapple into a bowl, add the cinnamon and chili powder, and stir to combine.

Transfer to a plate and serve with the coconut milk yogurt and a squeeze of lime juice.

Super Greens Smoothie Bowl ▶

Serves 1

½ avocado (pitted and skinned) | 1 small banana (peeled) | 1 generous handful of spinach | 1 handful of mung (or edamame) beans | 1 tsp almond nut butter | 1 tsp spirulina powder | squeeze of fresh lemon juice | ¼ tsp vanilla powder or seeds scraped from 1 vanilla bean | about ½ cup Cashew M*lk (see page 105) or Almond M*lk (see page 107) | blackberries or blueberries to decorate

Put all the ingredients, except the nutm*lk and berries, into a high-speed blender and pulse until you have a creamy texture. Add more or less of the specified quantity of nutm*lk to achieve the desired consistency. Pour into a bowl and decorate with the berries.

Raw Buckwheat Porridge

Serves 1

½ cup buckwheat groats | 1 tbsp almond or cashew nut butter | ½ cup Cashew M*lk (see page 105) or Almond M*lk (see page 107) | small cupped handful of blueberries to serve

Soak the groats in filtered water overnight. In the morning, drain and rinse through a sieve, then drain again. Add to a small food processor with the remaining ingredients and pulse until you have a smooth, creamy oatmeal-like texture. Serve with the blueberries.

Gluten-free Granola

Serves 3–4

1 cup gluten-free organic oats (or ½ cup each of oats and buckwheat flakes) |
1 generous handful each of raw cashew nuts, almonds, and pecan nuts |
1 tbsp melted ghee or coconut oil | 1 tsp vanilla powder or seeds scraped
from 1 vanilla bean | 1 heaping tbsp maca powder | 3 tbsp shredded coconut |
pinch of Himalayan salt | nutm*lk or dairy-free coconut milk yogurt to serve

Preheat the oven to 400°F. Line a baking sheet or large flat ovenproof
dish with nonstick parchment paper. Add the oats (or oats and
buckwheat mix) and nuts to the lined baking sheet or dish and mix
through the melted ghee or coconut oil and vanilla. Bake for about
20 minutes, stirring occasionally.

Remove from the oven, and let cool then mix through the maca, coconut,
and salt. Serve with a plant-based m*lk (I like cashew best — see page
105) or coconut milk yogurt. You can store the granola in an airtight jar
for up to 3–4 weeks.

Portobello Stack

Serves 1

1 tsp unsweetened organic Dijon mustard | 1 tsp dried thyme | 1 tsp
nutritional yeast flakes | 1 Portobello mushroom (stem removed) |
5 cherry tomatoes | ½ avocado | pinch of Himalayan salt | 1 tsp pumpkin
seeds to garnish | arugula salad to serve

Mix the mustard, thyme, and nutritional yeast together and spread
over the gills side of the mushroom. Put both the mushroom and the
tomatoes under a preheated medium broiler for about 10 minutes,
checking regularly so that they don't burn. Meanwhile, pit, skin, and
slice the avocado.

Remove the mushroom and tomatoes from the broiler. Place the
mushroom on a plate as a base, then top with the avocado slices and
tomatoes, sprinkle with the salt and sprinkle over the pumpkin seeds to
garnish. Serve with an arugula salad.

Sesame Sweet Potato and Kale with Tahini Dressing

Serves 2

1 medium-large sweet potato | 7–8 kale leaves | 1 tbsp tahini | 1 tbsp fresh lemon juice | a little coconut oil | 1 small red onion (finely sliced) | 1 garlic clove (crushed) | 2 tbsp sesame seeds | pinch of Himalayan salt

Preheat the oven to 400°F.

Peel and cut the sweet potato into relatively small chunks. Place on a baking sheet lined with nonstick parchment paper and bake for about 25 minutes until tender.

While the sweet potato is baking, trim the stems from the kale and put the leaves to one side. Make the dressing by simply whisking together the tahini, lemon juice, and enough water to thin to the right consistency — you don't want this too watery.

Heat a small amount of coconut oil in a skillet, add the onion, and stir-fry for 5 minutes. Add the garlic and cook for another 5 minutes, then stir in the kale and baked sweet potato and cook for another 2 minutes.

Take off the heat, stir in the tahini dressing, sprinkle with the sesame seeds and salt, and serve.

Ultimate Leafy Greens

Serves 1

1 generous handful each of kale (stems removed), baby spinach, arugula, and mung bean, lentil, or alfalfa sprouts (or a mixture) | 1 tbsp pumpkin seed oil (or olive oil) | fresh lemon juice | Himalayan salt

Combine the kale, spinach, arugula, and sprouts together in a large bowl. Dress with the pumpkin seed oil and lemon juice to taste, and season to taste with salt. *Voilà!*

Avocado, Radish, and Spinach Quinoa Salad

Serves 2

½ cup quinoa | 2 cups water | 1 avocado | 8–10 red radishes | 2 generous handfuls of baby spinach | 2 tbsp olive oil | 2 tbsp fresh lemon juice | 1 tsp ground cumin | ¼ tsp mustard powder | pinch of Himalayan salt and freshly ground black pepper

Rinse and drain the quinoa, then put into a saucepan with the water and bring to a boil, then reduce the heat, cover and simmer for about 10 minutes, until all of the water has been absorbed and the quinoa has cooked through (you may need to add some more water). Let cool; this salad can be served warm or at room temperature.

While the quinoa is cooling, halve the avocado and discard the pit, then remove the skin from the halves and slice the flesh. Wash, trim, and thinly slice the radishes.

Stir the avocado, radishes, and spinach through the quinoa. Whisk together the olive oil, lemon juice, cumin, mustard powder, and salt and pepper and use to dress the salad.

Avocado, Kale, and Hemp Hearts Salad

Serves 1

2 cups kale | ½ avocado | 1 generous handful of lentil sprouts (or other sprouts shoots such as mung bean sprouts or broccoli sprouts) | 1 tbsp hemp oil (or olive oil) | 1 tbsp cider vinegar | 1 tbsp hemp hearts (shelled hemp seeds) to garnish

Trim the stems from the kale and shred the leaves into smaller pieces. Add to a bowl.

Pit and skin the avocado, then slice into ½in thick pieces and add to the bowl along with the sprouts.

Whisk the oil and vinegar together to make a dressing and stir through the salad. Garnish with the hemp hearts and serve.

Rainbow Slaw ▶

Serves 1

½ cup each of shredded red cabbage, shredded white cabbage, and finely sliced fennel | ¼ small red onion (finely sliced) | 1 generous handful of cilantro (coarsely chopped) | 1 tsp finely chopped chile | 1 tsp tahini | 1 tsp cashew nut butter | pinch of Himalayan salt |squeeze of fresh lime juice | 1 tbsp raw cashew nuts to serve

Place the cabbage, fennel, onion, cilantro, and chile in a bowl and toss to combine.

To make the dressing, whisk the tahini, cashew nut butter, salt, and lime juice together in a bowl, adding water to thin. Stir into the slaw and serve sprinkled with the cashews.

Cauliflower Tabbouleh

Serves 2

1 head cauliflower (trimmed and coarsely chopped into smaller florets) | 10–12 cherry tomatoes (quartered) | 2 scallions (finely sliced) | 1 cup curly parsley (coarsely chopped) | 2 tbsp sunflower seeds | 1 tbsp fresh lemon juice | 1 tbsp olive oil | pinch of Himalayan salt

Pulse the cauliflower in a food processor until you get a fine couscous-type texture. Transfer to a large bowl.

Add the tomatoes, scallions, parsley, and sunflower seeds to the couscous. Dress with the lemon juice, oil, and salt and stir to combine all together. Serve!

Moroccan Spicy Carrots and Beet with Paprika Hummus

Serves 2

1 medium-large raw beet or 2 small ready-cooked organic beets | 4 carrots | 1 tsp coconut oil or ghee | 1 garlic clove (crushed or finely chopped) | 1 tsp ras el hanout | 1 tsp cumin seeds | 1 generous handful of mint (coarsely chopped) | 1 tbsp fresh lemon juice | 1 small handful of pistachio nuts | Himalayan salt and freshly ground black pepper | organic hummus and paprika to serve

Wash the raw beet well and trim, then place in a saucepan covered with water. Bring to a boil, then reduce the heat and simmer for about 1 hour, until cooked through, topping up the water if necessary. Remove from heat and leave until cool enough to handle, then peel away the skin and cut into small chunks.

If using cooked beet, simply remove from pack, chop each into 6–8 chunks, and put to one side.

Peel the carrots and slice into 5in batons. Steam for 5 minutes or cook in a saucepan of boiling water for 1–2 minutes so that they are still firm and put to one side.

Heat the coconut oil or ghee in a skillet and gently cook the garlic, ras el hanout, and cumin seeds for a few minutes. Add the beet and carrots and combine.

Remove from the heat and add the mint and lemon juice, season to taste with salt and pepper and stir through. Divide between two plates, sprinkle with the pistachio nuts and serve with a dollop of organic hummus sprinkled with paprika.

Roasted Red Pepper and Lima Bean Quinoa Salad

Serves 3–4

²/₃ cup dried lima beans or 15oz can lima beans (drained) | 2 red bell peppers | 4 tbsp cold-pressed organic olive oil | ½ cup quinoa | 2 cups water | 2 tbsp finely chopped parsley | 2 tbsp finely chopped chives | 1 tbsp fresh lemon juice | red pepper flakes (if you want an extra kick) | Himalayan salt and cracked black pepper

If using dried beans, soak them overnight in filtered water, then drain, rinse and drain again. Add to a large saucepan of water and bring to a boil, then reduce the heat, cover and simmer for about 1 hour. Drain and put to one side.

Preheat the oven to 400°F. Cut the peppers in half and remove the cores and seeds. Drizzle with the oil and sprinkle with salt to taste, then roast for about 20 minutes, turning once. Alternatively, you can cook them under the broiler to give the skins a more charred taste. Remove from the oven or broiler and let cool.

Rinse and drain the quinoa, then put into a large saucepan with the water and bring to a boil, then reduce the heat, cover, and simmer for about 10 minutes until all of the water has been absorbed and the quinoa has cooked through (you may need to add some more water). Let cool.

Slice the peppers and add to the quinoa, along with the cooked or canned lima beans and all the remaining ingredients. Season to taste with salt and cracked black pepper and toss together.

Celeriac, Wilted Chard, and Hazelnut Lentils

Serves 2

1 celeriac (you want about 2 cups, peeled and cut into 1in cubes | ¾ cup dried Puy lentils | 1 tsp ghee | 1 garlic clove (crushed) | 1 tbsp chopped tarragon | 4–5 chard leaves (trimmed and coarsely chopped) | 1 tsp capers (rinsed) | 2 tsp olive oil | 1 tsp cider vinegar | 8 hazelnuts (coarsely chopped)

Either lightly steam the celeriac for 10 minutes or place on a baking sheet lined with nonstick parchment paper and bake in an oven preheated to 400°F for 40 minutes.

Meanwhile, rinse the lentils and put in a small saucepan with water to cover. Bring to a boil, then reduce the heat, cover and simmer for about 30 minutes until tender, adding extra water if needed.

Once the celeriac and lentils have finished cooking, put to one side.

Heat the ghee in a saucepan, add the garlic and cook for a few minutes. Stir in the lentils, celeriac, tarragon, and chard. Remove from the heat and add the capers, olive oil, and vinegar. Serve sprinkled with the chopped hazelnuts.

Broccoli and Almond Soup

Serves 2

1 head broccoli (cut into mini florets) | 1 onion (quartered) | 2 garlic cloves (peeled) | 1 cup vegetable stock | 1 cup hot water | 1 tbsp almond nut butter | 1 tbsp olive oil | crushed almonds to garnish

Preheat the oven to 400°F. Line a baking sheet or flat ovenproof dish with nonstick parchment paper.

Spread the broccoli, onion, and garlic cloves out on the lined baking sheet or dish. Bake for about 20 minutes, until tender.

Transfer the roasted veggies to a blender with the stock, hot water, almond nut butter, and oil. Blitz until pureed and serve garnished with crushed almonds.

Miso Sesame Carrots and Leeks with Black Beans

Serves 2

4 small-medium carrots (peeled and sliced) | 2 leeks (sliced) | 15oz can black beans (drained) | 2 tbsp sweet white miso paste | 2 tsp mirin | 2 tsp tamari | 2 tsp cold-pressed sesame oil | pinch of Himalayan salt | 2 tsp sesame seeds

Lightly steam the carrots and leeks for about 6 minutes, until they are al dente.
Transfer to a bowl and stir through the beans, miso paste, mirin, and tamari. Drizzle over the sesame oil and season with the salt.
Sprinkle with the sesame seeds and serve.

Zucchinetti with Cashew Pesto

Serves 2

2 zucchini | squeeze of fresh lemon juice | pinch of Himalayan salt | 2 cups basil leaves | ¼ cup raw cashew nuts | ¼ cup pine nuts | 1 garlic clove (peeled) | ½ cup olive oil

Place the zucchini in a spiralizer to create the spaghetti. Mix with the lemon juice and salt in a bowl, then put to one side.

To make the cashew pesto, put the basil, cashews, pine nuts, and garlic into a small food processor and whiz to combine, gradually adding the oil while the machine is running.

Serve the zucchinetti with a generous spoonful of the pesto. You can keep the remainder in an airtight container in the fridge for up to five days.

index

acid reflux 15
acidic foods 17, 18
acne 38, 52
adrenal fatigue 26, 34–5
adrenaline 17, 31
Alkaline Iced Coffee 106
alkilinity 17–19
Almond M*lk 107
almonds 47, 50
  Broccoli and Almond Soup 116, 135
  Gluten-free Granola 120, 126
aloe vera juice 53
antibiotics 7, 8
antioxidants 33, 41, 47
apples 29, 41, 53, 59
  Apple and Ginger Bircher Muesli 116, 123
  Cholesterol Police 91
  Clean Roots 100
  Detox in the City 67
  Drink Your Salad 69
  FAB (Fennel, Apple, and Beet) 81
  Ginger CAM 89
  Ginger PAM 88
  Green Glow-getter 53, 69
  Minty Apple 85
  Purple CAG 99
  Smooth Move 29, 93
  Yamapple 96
arthritis 27, 48–9, 66
asparagus 47
asthma 38
avocados 31, 39, 47, 48
  Avocado, Kale, and Hemp Hearts Salad
    120, 129
  Avocado, Radish, and Spinach Quinoa Salad
    116, 129
  Super Greens Smoothie Bowl 120, 124

bananas 50
  Super Greens Smoothie Bowl 120, 124
basil 41
  Cholesterol Police 91
  Zucchinetti with Cashew Pesto 137
Beachside Popeye 64

beans
  Miso Sesame Carrots and Leeks with Black Beans
    120, 137
  Roasted Red Pepper and Lima Bean Quinoa
    Salad 120, 134
Beetbox 97
beets 33, 37, 47
  Beetbox 97
  Clean Roots 100
  and cleanse program symptoms 121
  FAB (Fennel, Apple, and Beet) 81
  Fitness Fuel 47, 75
  Gout Getter 37, 99
  Hypertension Hero 43, 100
  Liver Supporter 97
  Moroccan Spicy Carrots and Beet with Paprika
    Hummus 116, 133
  Spicy Beetroot Salad 75
beet greens 35
beet juice 43
beta-carotene 41
Black and Blue Salad 86
blood pH 17, 29
  testing 19
blood sugar 24, 30–1, 34
blueberries
  Black and Blue Salad 86
bok choy 47
brain
  and the digestive system 15
Brain-boosting Greens 69
Brazil nuts 39
broccoli 31, 43, 47, 48, 49, 50, 53
  Broccoli and Almond Soup 116, 135
  Green Glow-getter 53, 69
  Green Recovery 47, 64
  Hypertension Hero 43, 100
  Sweet Sexy Green 66
  Tropical Greens 49, 66
buckwheat
  Gluten-free Granola 120, 126
  Raw Buckwheat Porridge 116, 124
butternut squash 53

cabbage 48
  Purple CAG 99
  Rainbow Slaw 120, 130
Cacao Cashew M*lk 106
caffeine 50, 51
cancer 17
  and phytonutrients 22
  and sugar 24
carbohydrates 24, 30, 46
cardiovascular disease 40, 44, 50
Carotene Cuties 97
carrot juice 29
carrots 41, 53
  Beetbox 97
  Carotene Cuties 97
  Cholesterol Police 91
  Green and Orange 66
  Liver Supporter 97
  Miso Sesame Carrots and Leeks with Black Beans 120, 137
  Moroccan Spicy Carrots and Beet with Paprika Hummus 116, 133
  Self Tanner 90
  Smooth Move 29, 93
cashew nuts 50, 53
  Apple and Ginger Bircher Muesli 116, 123
  Cacao Cashew M*lk 106
  Cashew Nutm*lk 105
  Gluten-free Granola 120, 126
  Rainbow Slaw 120, 130
  Zucchinetti with Cashew Pesto 137
cauliflower 48
  Cauliflower Tabbouleh 120, 130
cayenne pepper 31
Celeriac, Wilted Chard, and Hazelnut lentils 116, 135
celery 35, 37, 43, 45, 49
  Brain-boosting Greens 69
  Detox in the City 67
  Gout Getter 37, 99
  Hypertension Hero 43, 100
  Minty Apple 85
  Snake Charmer 80
  Tropical Greens 49, 66
cell renewal 55
centifrugal juicers 56–7
chard 47, 53

Celeriac, Wilted Chard, and Hazelnut Lentils 116, 135
  Green Recovery 47, 64
cherries 37
  Gout Getter 37, 99
  sour cherry juice 51
chewing food 15
chia seeds 47, 53
chicken 50
chickpeas 50
chiles 53
chlorophyll 14, 19, 20
cholesterol levels 27, 40–1, 44
Cholesterol Police 91
cilantro 53
  Rainbow Slaw 120, 130
cinnamon 31
  Cinnamon-spiced Pineapple with Coconut Yogurt 116, 123
citrus fruits
  juicing 66
Clean Roots 100
cleanses 20, 56, 109–21
  benefits of 111
  cautionary note 111
  defining a cleanse 110
  and detoxification 110
  pantry makeover 112
  post-cleanse 120
  pre-cleanse 112, 116–17
  program 8, 30, 112–13
    cheat sheet 119
    cleanse day 118–19
    levels 110, 113
    number of days 110
    numbered juices 113, 118
    symptoms experienced during 121
coconut milk yogurt
  Cinnamon-spiced Pineapple with Coconut Yogurt 116, 123
coconut oil 41
coconut water 64
  Beachside Popeye 64
  Green Coco 65
  Green Recovery 47, 64
  Thai Melon Brightener 72
coffee
  and the pre-cleanse program 117

cold presses 56
colon
  and the digestive system 16
complex carbohydrates 24
constipation 27, 28–9
cortisol 17, 31, 34, 50
Craving Killa 31, 89
cucumber 47, 53
  Detox in the City 67
  Drink Your Salad 69
  Ginger CAM 89
  Green Coco 65
  Green Glow-getter 53, 69
  Greens and Grapes 91
  juicing 58
  Sweet Sexy Green 66
  Thai Melon Brightener 72
  Watermelon Green Patch 68

dandelion greens 53
depression 7, 14, 27, 34, 50
Detox in the City 67
detoxification 38, 44, 110
  liver 32, 33
  skin 53
diabetes 24, 25, 34, 38, 50
diarrhea 121
digestive system 14–16, 52
dopamine 31
Drink Your Salad 69

eczema 38, 52
eggs 50
Einstein, Albert 7–8, 9
endometriosis 38
endorphins 31
enzymes 15
excess weight 27, 30–1
exercise 17, 50

FAB (Fennel, Apple, and Beet) 81
fats in the diet 30
  good fats 115
fennel 53
  Detox in the City 67
  FAB (Fennel, Apple, and Beet) 81
  Green Glow-getter 53, 69
  Rainbow Slaw 120, 130

fertility and conception 38–9, 81
fiber 29, 55
figs 47
Fitness Fuel 47, 75
fitness performance 27, 46–7, 75
flax seeds (linseeds) 29, 41, 46, 48, 53
folic acid 37
free radicals 16, 17, 41
fructose (fruit sugar) 24–5
fruits
  GI levels 25
  for juicing 57, 59
  and pesticides 57
  and phytonutrients 22
Fruity Pep 39, 81

GI (glycemic index) 25, 59
ginger 47
  Apple and Ginger Bircher Muesli 116, 123
  Brain-boosting Greens 69
  Ginger CAM 89
  Ginger PAM 88
  Greens and Grapes 91
  Purple CAG 99
glucose 24
Gluten-free Granola 120, 126
gout 27, 36–7
Gout Getter 37, 99
grapefruit 31
  Craving Killa 31, 89
  Green and Orange 66
grapes
  Greens and Grapes 91
Green Coco 64
Green Glow-getter 53, 69
green juices 56
Green and Orange 66
Green Recovery 47, 64
green tea 31, 117
green vegetables 33, 47
  chlorophyll in 19, 20
  for juicing 57, 58
Greens and Grapes 91

hazelnuts 41
  Celeriac, Wilted Chard, and Hazelnut Lentils 116, 135
headaches 121

heart disease 22, 34, 40
hemoglobin 20
hemp hearts
  Avocado, Kale, and Hemp Hearts Salad
    120, 129
herbal teas 29
HFCS (high fructose corn syrup) 24
high blood pressure see hypertension
Himalayan salt 47, 115
homocysterine 34
hummus
  Moroccan Spicy Carrots, and Beet with Paprika
    Hummus 116, 133
hunger 15
hypertension 22, 27, 42–3
Hypertension Hero 43, 100
hypoglycemia 50

immune system 34, 50
inner physician 9, 11
insomnia 27, 50–1, 74
insulin 24, 25, 30, 31, 34
iron 47
Italian Savory Feast 74

juicers 56–7
juicing
  buying produce for 57
  and chlorophyl 20
  health benefits of 55
  and raw food 21
  tips for making juice 61

kale
  Avocado, Kale, and Hemp Hearts Salad
    120, 129
  Detox in the City 67
  Green Coco 65
  Green and Orange 66
  health benefits of 33, 48, 49, 51, 53, 58
  Liver Supporter 97
  Sesame Sweet Potato and Kale with Tahini
    Dressing 116, 127
  Tropical Greens 49, 66
  Ultimate Leafy Greens 116, 127
  Watermelon Green Patch 68
Kale Mary 76
Kalinik, Eve 12, 36, 46, 49, 50, 52

kiwi fruit 35
  Stress Buster 85

leeks
  Miso Sesame Carrots and Leeks with Black Beans
    120, 137
lemons
  hot water and lemon 117
  lemon juice 33
  Spicy Limonade 86
lentils 45
  Celeriac, Wilted Chard, and Hazelnut Lentils 116,
    135
lettuce 37, 47, 51
  Detox in the City 67
  Drink Your Salad 69
  Gout Getter 37, 99
  Green Recovery 47, 64
limes
  Green Coco 65
Little Green Book of Experts 11–13
liver function 15, 29
  fatigue 27, 32–3
  and fertility 38
Liver Supporter 97

maca 39, 45
masticating juicers 57
meditation 17
melatonin 50, 51
Mellow Garden 51, 74
melons
  Self Tanner 90
  Thai Melon Brightener 72
menus
  post-cleanse 120
  pre-cleanse 116
Mexican Mamacita 73
mint
  Ginger CAM 89
  Ginger PAM 88
  Watermelon Green Patch 68
Minty Apple 85
Miso Sesame Carrots and Leeks with Black Beans
  120, 137
Moroccan Spicy Carrots and Beets with Paprika
  Hummus 116, 133
mouth

and the digestive system 15
mung beans
  Ultimate Leafy Greens 116, 127
mushrooms
  Portobello Stack 120, 126

NO (nitrix oxide) 45
Norton, Henrietta 13, 38, 39
Norwalk Juicers 56
nutm*lks 104–7, 115
nutritional therapy 8, 12, 13

OA (osteoarthritis) 48–9
oats
  Apple and Ginger Bircher Muesli 116, 123
  Gluten–free Granola 120, 126
okra 47
oleic acid 31
oranges 35
  Green and Orange 66
  Stress Buster 85
  Turmeric Tonic 93
oxygen 20

papayas 29
  Smooth Move 29, 93
parsley 43
  Hypertension Hero 43, 100
PCOS (polycystic ovary syndrome) 38
Peacock, Gabriela 12, 24, 30, 34
pears 59
  Brain-boosting Greens 69
  FAB (Fennel, Apple, and Beet) 81
  Green Coco 65
  Sweet Sexy Green 66
pesticides 57
phytonutrients 14, 22, 29, 31
pineapple 49, 59
  Cinnamon-spiced Pineapple with Coconut Yogurt
    116, 123
  Ginger PAM 88
  Pineapple Power 82
  Tropical Greens 49, 66
PMS (premenstrual syndrome) 38
pomegranates 45
  Snake Charmer 80
Portobello Stack 120, 126
Pressed Juice Directory 56

probiotics 9
protein 30, 46
psoriasis 52
psyllium husks 29, 31
Pulichino, Romina 11, 15, 45, 80
pumpkin seeds 39, 53
Purple CAG 99

quinoa
  Avocado, Radish, and Spinach Quinoa Salad
    116, 129

Rad Green Juice 64
radishes
  Avocado, Radish, and Spinach Quinoa Salad
    116, 129
Rainbow Savory Dinner 73
Rainbow Slaw 120, 130
raspberries 39
raw buckwheat porridge 116, 124
raw foods 21
relaxation 35
rhubarb
  Strawberry Rhubarb Tart 86

Savory Green 76
Self Tanner 90
serotonin 8, 16, 31, 34
sesame seeds 47, 50
  Sesame Sweet Potato, and Kale with Tahini
    Dressing 116, 127
sexual dysfunction 27, 44–5, 80
simple carbohydrates 24
skin health 27, 52-3, 69
sleep
  and adrenal fatigue 34
  see also insomnia
sleep apnea 50
small intestine
  and the digestive system 15
Smooth Move 29, 93
Snake Charmer 45, 80
social plans
  and cleansing 118–19
soluble fiber 29, 55
soy protein 41
Spicy Beet Salad 75
Spicy Limonade 86

spinach
  Avocado, Radish, and Spinach Quinoa Salad 116, 129
  Clean Roots 100
  Green and Orange 66
  health benefits of 43, 45, 47, 48, 49, 51, 53, 58
  Snake Charmer 80
  Sweet Sexy Green 66
  Tropical Greens 49, 66
  Ultimate Leafy Greens 116, 127
spirulina 31
stomach
  and the digestive system 15
Strawberry Rhubarb Tart 86
stress and adrenal fatigue 26, 34–5
Stress Buster 85
sucrose 24
sugar 24–5, 30
sugar snap peas
  Savory Green 76
Super Greens Smoothie Bowl 120, 124
sweet peppers 39, 48, 53
  Fruity Pep 81
  Roasted Red Pepper and Lima Bean Quinoa Salad 120, 134
  Self Tanner 90
sweet potatoes 53
  Carotene Cuties 97
  Sesame Sweet Potato and Kale with Tahini Dressing 116, 127
  Yamapple 96
Sweet Sexy Green 66

Talib, Dr. Nigma 13, 40, 41, 42
Thai Melon Brightener 72
tomato juice 43

tomatoes
  Cauliflower Tabbouleh 120, 130
  Portobello Stack 120, 126
Tropical Greens 49, 66
turmeric 33, 41
  Turmeric Tonic 93

Ultimate Leafy Greens 116, 127

vegetables
  cholesterol lowering 41
  for juicing 57, 58–9
  and pesticide 57
  and phytonutrients 22
vertical slow juicers 57
vitamin A 53
vitamin B6 41
vitamin C 35, 39, 48, 53, 59
vitamin D 48
vitamin E 39, 48
vomiting 121

water intake 29, 118
watermelons 45
  Snake Charmer 80
  Watermelon Green Patch 68
wheatgrass 37
  Pineapple Power 82

Yamapple 96

zinc 53
  deficiency 39
zucchini
  Brain-boosting Greens 69
  Zucchinetti with Cashew Pesto 137

Bibliography

Page 20: "A 13-week subchronic toxicity study of sodium iron chlorophyllin in F344 rats"; *The Journal of Toxicological Sciences*, Vol.39, No. 1, 2014.

Page 43: "Dietary Approach to Attenuate Oxidative Stress, Hypertension and Inflammation in the Cardiovascular System"; *Proceedings of the National Academy of Sciences of the USA*, Vol.101, 2004.

Acknowledgments

Kara's thanks go to...

My husband Leon who bore with me typing through nights and weekends while writing this book. You are my rock, my inspiration, and my best taste tester. I wouldn't want to do any of it without you. I love you. My daughter Belle (pictured above) who more than ever made me think about how every morsel that goes into your mouth has the potential to build your healthy future. It's never felt more important since you made me a mama! My parents Patti and Steve who, in addition to always making me feel loved, made me sit down for a "proper" home made meal, never let me eat sugar cereal or chew sugar gum. As much as I screamed about it growing up, I thank you today! My rockstar friends and bestest recipe tasters Charlotte "Mamaganoush" Knight and Lucy "tastemaker" Thomas. You are hellava more than taste buds to me. Thank you for always having my back (and sides, too!). Jenna Zoe, thank you for believing in me, and letting me start PLENISH in a corner of your kitchen in return for Mind Body Green juice. Thank you also for my addiction to Upcakes peanut butter cups. Vicky Bond and Emma Sinclair, thank you for showing a UK newbie like me the British ropes and inspiring me! Calgary Avansino, thank you for being a green trailblazer and our gorgeous loudspeaker when everyone was still wondering what that weird green liquid we were trying to get everyone drinking was! All of the brilliant experts, Eve Kalinik, Romi Pulichino, Gabriela Peacock, Dr. Nigma Talib, and Henrietta Norton, thank you for sharing your expertise. You've inspired me, and I know your knowledge will touch the lives of many others. Keep spreading your green love! To the PLENISH team, thank you for keeping the ship moving full-steam ahead during my absence. You are my most valuable assets. And finally, Stephanie Jackson who, in a moment of craziness, let me convince her to publish this book. Yasia Williams and Polly Poulter, I am super grateful for your help — we are all birthing this baby of a book together. Puuuusssh!!!!

Publishing Director: Stephanie Jackson
Editor: Pollyanna Poulter
Deputy Art Director: Yasia Williams
Illustration & Design: Abigail Read
Photography: Mowie Kay
Prop Stylist: Iris Bromet
Home Economist (food recipes): Lucy Thomas
Indexer: Isobel McLean
Americanizer: Nicole Foster
Assistant Production Manager: Lucy Carter
Photo credits: page 117 Martin Lee/Alamy; cover, pages 2–3, 14, 18–19, 21, 22–23, 58–59, 62–63, 70–71, 78–79, 94–95, 102–103 Amber Locke @rawveganblonde